HSK 与《国际中文教育中文水平等级标准》对接研究——以 HSK5 写作为例

张新玲 项颖 著

东南大学出版社
SOUTHEAST UNIVERSITY PRESS
·南京·

图书在版编目(CIP)数据

HSK与《国际中文教育中文水平等级标准》对接研究：以HSK5写作为例/张新玲，项颖著. —南京：东南大学出版社，2023.12

ISBN 978-7-5766-0994-3

Ⅰ.①H… Ⅱ.①张… ②项… Ⅲ.①汉语—写作—对外汉语教学—研究 Ⅳ.①H195.3

中国国家版本馆CIP数据核字(2023)第223860号

责任编辑：陈淑 朱震霞　责任校对：张万莹　封面设计：王玥　责任印制：周荣虎

HSK与《国际中文教育中文水平等级标准》对接研究——以HSK5写作为例

HSK Yu《Guoji Zhongwen Jiaoyu Zhongwen Shuiping Dengji Biaozhun》Duijie Yanjiu——Yi HSK5 Xiezuo Wei Li

著　者	张新玲　项颖
出版发行	东南大学出版社
出 版 人	白云飞
社　　址	南京市四牌楼2号(邮编：210096)
网　　址	http://www.seupress.com
电子邮箱	press@seupress.com
经　　销	全国各地新华书店
印　　刷	广东虎彩云印刷有限公司
开　　本	700 mm×1000 mm　1/16
印　　张	13.75
字　　数	290千字
版　　次	2023年12月第1版
印　　次	2023年12月第1次印刷
书　　号	ISBN 978-7-5766-0994-3
定　　价	79.00元

本社图书若有印装质量问题，请直接与营销部联系，电话：025-83791830。

前　言

"语言的边界就是世界的边界",在以中国式现代化全面推进中华民族伟大复兴、构建中国自主知识体系和话语体系的百年未有之大变局背景下,我国汉语国际教育面临时代的挑战和崭新的发展机遇。2022年9月国务院学位委员会和教育部发布了《研究生教育学科专业目录(2022年)》《研究生教育学科专业目录管理办法》,首次将"汉语国际教育"与教育学、心理学、体育学等并列为教育学门类下的一级学科,凸显了百年未有之大变局下,汉语国际教育在中华文化复兴与中国文化传播中不可替代的价值。

同时,在全球化和逆全球化浪潮并行的历史时期,在向世界展示中国高等教育方案、扎实推进共建"一带一路"教育行动背景下,中国制定了汉语国际教育规范和标准——《国际中文教育中文水平等级标准》(简称《等级标准》)。该标准全面描述了外国中文学习者初、中、高三个阶段九个级别应达到的听、说、读、写、译等中文水平标准,对政策制定、教学实施、教材编写、考试和评价具有指导作用,HSK等汉语水平考试也不例外。在标准制定阶段,通过事前效度验证研究结果改进和完善量表是应有之义。

现行包含1~6六个级别的汉语水平考试(HSK)是全球最权威的国际汉语能力标准化考试。伴随着《等级标准》的发布实施,在原有HSK 1至6级的基础上,HSK 7至9级已面向全球施考(汉考国际,2023)。将考试与语言标准对接是解释考试分数的常用方法,对HSK考试和《等级标准》的对接研究成为关系考试改革走向的重大课题。迄今国内已有大部分研究聚焦英语水平考试与《欧洲语言共同参考框架:学习、教学、评估》(简称《欧框》)或《中国英语能力等级量表》的对接,但针对汉语国际教育领域重要能力标准和考试的对接研究却相当匮乏。鉴于HSK5级报考人数多、是很多学历项目和职业市场语言门槛的现实,本书内容将聚焦HSK5级和《等级标准》5级的对接研究。与此同时,考虑到学习者目的语交际语言能力测评中写作能力举足轻重的地位,以及写作能力发展难度大、一定程度上滞后于其他技能的发展、学术写作是中高级学习者的重要真实任务等因素,我们进一步将研究焦点缩小到5级写作能力上。

本书涵盖互相关联的两部分内容:第一部分聚焦《等级标准》5级写作能力描述语实证效度验证研究,第二部分聚焦HSK5与《等级标准》的对接研究。本书内容在一定程度上反映了中文国际教育标准和测试在"一带一路"建设中提升中文影响力方面的重要价值,主要体现在以下方面:(1)对HSK分数进行解释,HSK完善和改革;(2)对HSK和《等级标准》对接研究提供方法借鉴;(3)为全球各类相关办学机构、政府决策部门、孔子学院以及教育官员、家长、教师、学生、研究者等提供参考;(4)对中国高校海外办学的语言选择、汉语国际教育、汉语标准和考试世界品牌建设等也有一定的参考价值。

本书适用于国际中文教育政策制定者、教师等从业人员;语言学及应用语言学专业教师、学生、研究人员参考阅读。①

---

① 本研究得到"《汉语水平等级标准》项目实证研究"资助;部分数据由汉考国际(北京)有限公司授权使用,谨致谢忱。

目　录

第一部分:《国际中文教育中文水平等级标准》5 级写作能力描述语实证效度验证 ·········· 001
- 1　引言 ·········· 003
- 2　研究框架 ·········· 004
- 3　研究方法 ·········· 006
  - 3.1　问卷设计 ·········· 006
  - 3.2　数据收集 ·········· 007
  - 3.3　数据分析 ·········· 008
- 4　结果 ·········· 010
  - 4.1　学生问卷数据 ·········· 010
  - 4.2　教师问卷数据 ·········· 012
- 5　结论 ·········· 017

第二部分:Aligning HSK Level 5 Writing Test with *Chinese Proficiency Grading Standards for International Chinese Language Education*（HSK5 写作能力与《国际中文教育中文水平等级标准》的对接研究） ·········· 021
- 6　Introduction ·········· 023
  - 6.1　Research Background ·········· 023
  - 6.2　Research Objectives ·········· 026
  - 6.3　Research Significance ·········· 027
- 7　Literature Review ·········· 029
  - 7.1　Aligning Tests with Language Standards ·········· 029
  - 7.2　*Chinese Proficiency Grading Standards for International Chinese Language Education* ·········· 041
  - 7.3　Hanyu Shuiping Kaoshi（HSK） ·········· 051
  - 7.4　Research Questions ·········· 058

		7.5	Summary	059
8	Methodology			061
		8.1	Working Theoretical Framework	061
		8.2	Research Design	063
		8.3	Data Collection	079
		8.4	Data Analysis	080
9	Results			082
		9.1	Results for Research Question One	082
		9.2	Results for Research Question Two	088
		9.3	Results for Research Question Three	105
		9.4	Results for Research Question Four	137
10	Discussion			159
		10.1	Discussion on the Content Alignment	159
		10.2	Discussion on the Performance Standards	167
11	Conclusion			173
		11.1	The Major Findings of the Present Study	173
		11.2	Implications of the Present Study	176
		11.3	Limitations and Directions for Further Research	177

Appendices ········ 187

第一部分

《国际中文教育中文水平等级标准》
5级写作能力描述语实证效度验证

1 引 言

2021年3月,《国际中文教育中文水平等级标准》(中华人民共和国教育部等,2021)(简称《等级标准》)正式发布,《等级标准》是描述全球汉语学习者所能达到的目标语言水平的国家级标准,是全球汉语国际教育教学和考试等环节的指导性标准,也是教育官员、专家、教师、学生、考试分数用户等利益相关人的重要参考文件。其发布实施是落实"十四五"国家发展规划中所列构建国际中文教育标准体系的具体举措,将在教学、测评和社会应用的各相关领域产生极大影响,其质量至关重要。

同时,效度良好的语言能力量表是编制好的语言测试的必要条件,如果语言量表的效度不理想,会导致基于该量表的测验效度不高。比如,已有多个语种的国际语言测试项目采用关联一定语言能力量表的成绩报告单,以便利益相关人对该成绩单上的成绩进行解释。进行效度验证是学界和国际量表研制领域的通用做法(Berger,2020;Alderson,2007;Wisniewski,2018;方绪军 等,2017;刘建达 等,2017;曾用强,2020)。

因此,开展效度验证工作对《等级标准》的制定意义重大。考虑到以下原因,本研究将聚焦《等级标准》5级写作描述语效度验证:(1) 以5级为中间代表的国际中文学习中等水平成就,体现在语言学习成就需求、成功的学习者数量、中国高等院校留学生入学的语言门槛、外国人进入中资公司和中国就业市场的语言门槛等方面;(2) 写作能力是语言学习者交际语言能力的重要、核心要素,具有举足轻重的作用。本研究有望推进《等级标准》建设,可成为《等级标准》面向全球发布前后为研究界、业界、学生、家长提供科学解释的重要参考。

2 研究框架

效度(validity)是教育测量中最重要的概念之一,效度理论经历了从"分类效度观"到"整体效度观"的发展。根据分类效度观的主张,效度可被分解为构念效度、内容效度、效标关联效度等类型(Cronbach,1998)。整体效度观认为"对经验证据和理论依据在多大程度上支持分数的解释与使用进行的综合评价就是效度",包括效度的内容、实质、结构、概化、外推、后效6个方面(Messicks,1989)。整体效度观具有"一元多维"的核心地位,为美国教育研究协会、心理学协会和教育测量学会制定的《教育与心理测量标准》所采用(AERA et al.,2014)。

就效度验证而言,凯恩(Kane,1992)提出"基于论证的效验模式",包括两个步骤:明确效度验证观点、收集有关证据。巴克曼(Bachman)发展了凯恩的效度论证观,提出"测试使用论证框架"(Assessment Use Argument,AUA)。韦尔(Weir)从社会认知视角出发,提出"基于证据的效验框架"(Weir,2005),涵盖五个方面的效验证据:基于理论的效度、环境效度、评分效度、效标关联效度和后果效度,并将基于理论的效度更名为认知效度,受试特征也成为效验证据很重要的方面(Shaw & Weir, 2007; Khalifa & Weir, 2009; Taylor, 2011; Geranpayeh & Taylor, 2013)。本研究将在以上效度理论及效度验证框架下展开。

在所有效度验证的范式中,效度证据都处于核心地位。综合来看,效度证据大致可分为"理性"和"实证"两大类。前者基于学科理论知识,通过演绎、归纳、类比等思辨方法来论证假设(即构念);后者则通过田野调查、实验等方法来获得数据以验证假设。本研究聚焦5级写作能力描述语的实证效度验证工作。

从时间序列来看,效度证据可分为即时效度证据和延时效度证据两类。前者指在量表开发之初(构念描述阶段)或者开发过程中(量表编制阶段)收集到的效度证据,主要类型为构念效度(结构、内容)和公平效度证据。效度证据类型包括与量表语言能力构念有关的效度证据、与描述参数有关的效度证据、公平效度证据、描述语效度证据及划分效度证据等。量表应用阶段的即时效度证据以决策效度(效标关联效度)为主,主要证据为直接决策和间接决策中的效度证据。量表投入使用后,收集反拨效度和社会影响效度,效度证据可来自教育管理者、教师、学生、政府、企业、专家学者等。在延时效度研究阶段,也包括了类似的效度类型和效度证据类型,且时序性不明显。本研究是《等级标准》研发工作的有机组成部分,在时间序列上属于量表研制阶段的效度验证。

综上,本研究在测试使用论证框架指导下,立足事前实证效度验证,基于梅西克(Messicks)的整体效度观侧重其内容方面,结合巴克曼的测试使用论证框架(Bachman et al., 2010)和韦尔的社会认知视角(Piccardo et al., 2020;Weir, 2005)开展《等级标准》5级写作能力描述语的效度验证工作。采用定性和定量研究相结合的方法,主要从内容和结构效度的视角为《等级标准》描述语内容确定提供学科论证,旨在回答以下问题:(1)《等级标准》5级写作描述语的有效性如何?(2)《等级标准》5级写作能力因子与理论构念匹配程度如何?

3 研究方法

拟运用定性和定量相结合的思路,采用理论论述和问卷调查法,对《等级标准》5级写作能力的描述语进行效度验证。测试使用论证框架强调清楚描写期望效果,识别并列出利益相关人(Bachman et al.,2010)。《等级标准》开发之初设定5级写作能力为理论效度/认知效度;期望效果为《等级标准》描述语与汉语国际教育教师和学习者等利益相关人的判断一致,这也从一个侧面体现了任何社会活动的变迁均在语言上留下了痕迹(刘利,2021)。因此,我们拟通过调查汉语国际教师和学生对《等级标准》5级写作能力描述的认可程度来收集实证证据,开展效度验证工作。研究的基本假设是:如果《等级标准》中5级写作能力的描述语是有效的,那么来自核心利益相关人(学生和老师等)的调查数据应该支持这些描述,描述语效度理想;反之,那么来自他们的调查数据可能不支持这些描述,描述语有待改进。同时,不同来源(学生和老师)的实证证据在一定程度上确保数据三角互证。

3.1 问卷设计

本研究报告的5级写作能力问卷基于《国际中文教育中文等级水平标准》实证效度验证研究设计。项目组于2019年12月至2020年4月,结合《等级标准》描述内容,按不同级别、技能设计调查问卷,编制学生、教师、专家问卷共45套,并根据调查对象翻译成了英语、法语、西班牙语、日语、韩语、俄语、泰语、阿拉伯语等8个语种。

根据研究需要,单独设置了学生问卷和教师问卷。两个问卷设计的构念为《等级标准》中5级写作能力,旨在调查描述语与利益相关人判断的匹配程度。问卷由"知情同意书""问卷指导语""受试基本信息"和目标语言能力问卷题目构成。学生问卷针对5级写作设置10道题目,均以《等级标准》对应部分描述语为基础设计,采用李克特 5 点量表问卷法,其中选项意义如下:1=完全不符合、2=勉强符合、3=基本符合、4=比较符合、5=完全符合。教师问卷与学生问卷大部分内容相同,区别之处在于增加了 2 道开放性题目,即第 11 题(从您的教学经验来看,汉语学习者要达到《等级标准》5 级写作能力要求的难易程度如何?为什么?)和第 12 题(整体而言,您觉得本问卷中的描述语能不能反映具备 5 级中文水平的学习者在写作方面应达到的要求?您有何补充?)。

问卷初稿完成后,均进行了专家审阅、学生作答 2 轮试测。试测内容包括问卷结构是否合理、问卷题目表述是否明晰、受试是否能够理解问卷题目并恰当作答等。试测数据用于问卷修改,直至定稿。问卷定稿后,由汉考国家组织 8 个语种的相关专家对学生问卷进行了同步翻译,此项工作时间为 2020 年 3 月至 4 月。学生问卷共有中英、中日、中韩、中俄、中泰、中西、中阿、中法 8 个语种版本;教师问卷以中英文对照呈现。

3.2 数据收集

问卷数据收集工作由汉考国际协调完成。在正式发放问卷前,我们以中英双语学生问卷进行了先导实验,主要进行问卷数据收集流程等。按照描述语的暂定级别、描述语适合的目标群体,参照学习者中文水平确定问卷作答目标学生群体。先导研究为正式收集数据提供了改进方案。所有受试在完成问卷之前填写知情同意书,确认自愿受邀填写问卷。

正式问卷数据收集时间为 2020 年 4 月 25 日至 6 月 12 日,向中国汉语水平考试考点和学校及亚洲、欧洲、大洋洲等 6 个国家和地区发放涵盖 9 个等级的中英、中泰、中西、中日、中俄、中法、中阿、中韩 8 类双语问卷,共收到来自 37 个国家的有效学生问卷 2 520 份,来自汉语国际教育领域的有效专家问卷 81 份。276 位满足要求的学生受试和 85 名汉语国际教育教师受试分别有效完成了 5 级写作能力学生和教师问卷。

1) 学生受试

如前所述,共有 276 位来自 37 个国家和地区的学生受试受邀完成了不同语种的《等级标准》5 级写作能力标准的学生问卷。其中,52 位受试完成了

(18.84%)中英对照版、17位(6.16%)中泰语对照版、4位(1.45%)中西语对照版、30位(10.87%)中日语对照版、3位(1.09%)中俄语对照版、4位(1.45%)中法语对照版、40位(14.49%)中阿语对照版、126位(45.65%)中韩语对照版。

2) 教师受试

有效完成5级写作能力标准教师问卷的85名教师受试的性别、年龄、教龄、教育背景、研究方向、在中国(含港澳台地区)留学的经历、任教国家/地区、教学对象、所教多数学生母语等情况如下:按性别分,男性11位(12.94%),女性74位(87.06%);按教龄分,44位受试(51.76%)从教1—4年,18位受试(21.18%)5—8年,11位受试(12.94%)9—12年,12位受试(14.12%)12年以上;按教育背景分,专科及以下者2位(2.35%),大学本科学历33位(38.83%),硕士研究生学历48位(56.47%),博士研究生学历2位(2.35%);按研究方向分,中文类25位(29.41%)、其他方向60位(70.59%);按教师受试在中国(含港澳台地区)留学的经历分,从未在上述国家/地区留学者56位(65.88%),留学1年以下和5—6年者各1位(1.18%),10位(11.76%)留学1—4年,17位(20.00%)留学7—10年。

教师受试任教国家/地区如下:埃及17位(20.00%),俄罗斯5位(5.88%),法国2位(2.35%),韩国6位(7.06%),加拿大1位(1.18%),日本9位(10.59%),泰国17位(20.00%),西班牙28位(32.94%)。教师受试的教学对象包括:小学生及幼儿园学生为主13位(15.29%),初中生为主26位(30.59%),高中生为主7位(8.24%),大学生为主20位(23.53%),兴趣班和社会成员为主19位(22.35%)。教师受试所教多数学生的母语占比如下:阿拉伯语17人(20.00%),俄语5人(5.88%),法语2人(2.35%),韩语6人(7.06%),日语9人(10.59%),泰语16人(18.82%),西班牙语27人(31.76%),英语3人(3.54%)。

3.3 数据分析

研究主要采用描述性统计和二项式检验分析方法,对学生和教师问卷数据分别进行分析。描述性统计分析的基本假设是:在所有正向问卷题目中,学生应答数据值越大,代表其对该题目代表的《等级标准》描述语判断越正面,描述语效度越高,且学生汉语水平(技能)越高。在负向题中,学生应答数据值越大,代表其对该题目代表的《等级标准》描述语判断越负面,描述语效度越高,但学生汉语水平(技能)越低。

二项式检验主要用于推断5点量表中受试应答数据的分布情况,对问卷题目陈述的"赞同组"和"反对组"进行二项式检验。前者包括选项为4—5的受试组,后者选项为1—3的受试组。如果二项式检验发现两组之间有显著差异,则推断"赞同组"或"反对组"受试为多数,具有统计学意义。

4 结 果

4.1 学生问卷数据

表4.1显示5级写作能力标准学生问卷中5点量表题的描述性统计分析数值。分析显示,统计数据都呈正态分布(偏度和峰度均在-2—2区间内)、多数题目均值略高于3,标准差大约为1,最小值均为1,最大值均为5。

表4.1 5级写作能力学生问卷数据描述统计($n=276$)

项目	最小值	最大值	均值	标准偏差	偏度		峰度	
	统计	统计	统计	统计	统计	标准误差	统计	标准误差
第1题:我能分析常见汉字的结构	1	5	3.30	1.006	-0.156	0.147	-0.379	0.292
第2题:我能在规定时间内,使用较为复杂的句式进行书面的语段表达,完成一般的叙述、说明或简单的议论性语言材料,字数不低于450字	1	5	2.98	1.056	0.036	0.147	-0.612	0.292
第3题:我能在规定时间内,完成一般的叙述、说明或简单的议论性语言材料,用词较为恰当	1	5	3.04	0.986	-0.019	0.147	-0.433	0.292
第4题:我能在规定时间内,完成一般的叙述、说明或简单的议论性语言材料,句式基本正确	1	5	3.07	1.012	-0.118	0.147	-0.369	0.292
第5题:我能在规定时间内,完成一般的叙述、说明或简单的议论性语言材料,内容比较完整	1	5	3.05	1.038	0.009	0.147	-0.485	0.292

续表

项目	最小值 统计	最大值 统计	均值 统计	标准偏差 统计	偏度 统计	偏度 标准误差	峰度 统计	峰度 标准误差
第6题：我能在规定时间内，完成一般的叙述、说明或简单的议论性语言材料，表达比较清楚	1	5	3.05	1.013	0.081	0.147	−0.502	0.292
第7题：我能完成一般的应用文体写作，格式基本正确	1	5	3.05	1.024	0.049	0.147	−0.578	0.292
第8题：我能完成一般的应用文体写作，表达基本规范	1	5	3.10	0.971	0.059	0.147	−0.372	0.292
第9题：我能在规定时间内，使用语段完成简单的叙述和说明，字数不低于300字	1	5	3.08	1.068	−0.026	0.147	−0.541	0.292
第10题：我能在规定时间内，完成常见的多种应用文体的书面表达，字数不低于600字	1	5	2.91	1.098	0.039	0.147	−0.707	0.292

表4.2数据显示，所有量表题目二项式检验结果均＜0.05。结合上文描述性统计值，可初步得出结论，在本研究采样的受试范围内，《等级标准》5级写作能力"赞同组"人数均显著高于"反对组"人数，受试对5级写作能力标准学生问卷题目陈述内容总体持肯定态度，《等级标准》5级写作能力描述语总体效度较理想。

表4.2 5级写作能力标准学生问卷数据二项式检验结果($n=276$)

题目	组别	类别	个案数	实测比例	检验比例	精确显著性（双尾）
第1题	组1	2	116	0.42	0.50	0.010
	组2	1	160	0.58		
	总计		276	1.00		
第2题	组1	2	88	0.32	0.50	0.000
	组2	1	188	0.68		
	总计		276	1.00		
第3题	组1	2	89	0.32	0.50	0.000
	组2	1	187	0.68		
	总计		276	1.00		

续表

题目	组别	类别	个案数	实测比例	检验比例	精确显著性（双尾）
第4题	组1	2	92	0.33	0.50	0.000
	组2	1	184	0.67		
	总计		276	1.00		
第5题	组1	2	90	0.33	0.50	0.000
	组2	1	186	0.67		
	总计		276	1.00		
第6题	组1	2	89	0.32	0.50	0.000
	组2	1	187	0.68		
	总计		276	1.00		
第7题	组1	2	92	0.33	0.50	0.000
	组2	1	184	0.67		
	总计		276	1.00		
第8题	组1	2	90	0.33	0.50	0.000
	组2	1	186	0.67		
	总计		276	1.00		
第9题	组1	2	94	0.34	0.50	0.000
	组2	1	182	0.66		
	总计		276	1.00		
第10题	组1	2	85	0.31	0.50	0.000
	组2	1	191	0.69		
	总计		276	1.00		

4.2 教师问卷数据

表4.3显示5级写作能力标准教师问卷数据的描述性统计分析数值。统计数据都呈正态分布（偏度和峰度均在－2—2区间内）、均值位于3左右，标准差接近1，最小值均为1，最大值均为5。教师进行问卷填写的依据主要有：教学观察、学生通过HSK/HSKK考试级别、教材或者课程大纲、学生在真实场景中的语言运用情况、国际国内汉语教学实际状况、国际国内汉语学习者平均水

平等。

表 4.3　5 级写作能力标准教师问卷数据描述性统计结果（$n=85$）

项目	最小值 统计	最大值 统计	平均值 统计	标准差 统计	偏度 统计	偏度 标准误差	峰度 统计	峰度 标准误差
第1题：能分析常见汉字的结构	1	5	3.52	0.908	−0.249	0.261	−0.281	0.517
第2题：能在规定时间内，使用较为复杂的句式进行书面的语段表达，完成一般的叙述、说明或简单的议论性语言材料，字数不低于450字	1	5	3.08	0.903	−0.464	0.261	−0.501	0.517
第3题：能在规定时间内，完成一般的叙述、说明或简单的议论性语言材料，用词较为恰当	1	4	3.02	0.771	−0.360	0.261	−0.395	0.517
第4题：能在规定时间内，完成一般的叙述、说明或简单的议论性语言材料，句式基本正确	1	4	3.02	0.845	−0.409	0.261	−0.658	0.517
第5题：能在规定时间内，完成一般的叙述、说明或简单的议论性语言材料，内容比较完整	1	4	3.02	0.831	−0.300	0.261	−0.877	0.517
第6题：能在规定时间内，完成一般的叙述、说明或简单的议论性语言材料，表达比较清楚	1	4	3.08	0.805	−0.432	0.261	−0.586	0.517
第7题：能完成一般的应用文体写作，格式基本正确	1	5	3.09	0.895	−0.495	0.261	−0.410	0.517
第8题：能完成一般的应用文体写作，表达基本规范	1	5	3.05	0.844	−0.334	0.261	−0.328	0.517
第9题：能在规定时间内，使用语段完成简单的叙述和说明，字数不低于300字	1	4	3.15	0.866	−0.755	0.261	−0.185	0.517
第10题：能在规定时间内，完成常见的多种应用文体的书面表达，字数不低于600字	1	4	2.78	0.943	−0.231	0.261	−0.880	0.517

表 4.4 显示，进入此模型的李克特 5 点量表题目，二项式检验结果 $p=0.00$（<0.05）。结合上文描述性统计值，可初步得出结论，在本研究采样的受试范围内，教师受试对于《等级标准》5 级写作能力标准"赞同组"人数总体上显著高于"反对组"人数，受试对 5 级写作能力标准教师问卷题目陈述内容总体持肯定

态度,《等级标准》5 级写作能力描述语总体效度较理想。

表 4.4　5 级写作能力标准教师问卷数据二项式检验结果($n=85$)

题目	组别	类别	个案数	实测比例	检验比例	精确显著性(双尾)
第1题	组1	2	74	0.87	0.50	0.000
	组2	1	11	0.13		
	总计		85	1.00		
第2题	组1	2	63	0.74	0.50	0.000
	组2	1	22	0.26		
	总计		85	1.00		
第3题	组1	1	20	0.24	0.50	0.000
	组2	2	65	0.76		
	总计		85	1.00		
第4题	组1	1	23	0.27	0.50	0.000
	组2	2	62	0.73		
	总计		85	1.00		
第5题	组1	1	24	0.28	0.50	0.000
	组2	2	61	0.72		
	总计		85	1.00		
第6题	组1	2	65	0.76	0.50	0.000
	组2	1	20	0.24		
	总计		85	1.00		
第7题	组1	2	64	0.75	0.50	0.000
	组2	1	21	0.25		
	总计		85	1.00		
第8题	组1	1	21	0.25	0.50	0.000
	组2	2	64	0.75		
	总计		85	1.00		
第9题	组1	1	18	0.21	0.50	0.000
	组2	2	67	0.79		
	总计		85	1.00		

续表

题目	组别	类别	个案数	实测比例	检验比例	精确显著性(双尾)
第10题	组1	1	33	0.39	0.50	0.050
	组2	2	52	0.61		
	总计		85	1.00		

表4.5显示了教师受试对《等级标准》5级写作能力标准问卷第11题的应答数据。认为学习者要达到5级写作能力要求很难、比较难、有点难、不太难、容易的受试人数和百分比分别为3(3.53%)、33(38.82%)、11(12.94%)、6(7.06%)、2(2.35%),另有30位(35.29%)受试未作答。部分教师受试填写的主要原因见表4.5。

表4.5 5级写作能力标准教师问卷主观题数据(第11题)($n=85$)

难易度	人数（占比）	原因
难	3 (3.53%)	1. 学生们很难区别相似的形容词所对应的对象,翻译和意思相近的单词多,容易混用; 2. 学生需要语言文化的熏陶。但是目前的考试属于应试,部分学员能达到这个水平,而且不用就会忘
比较难/不容易	33 (38.82%)	1. 对词汇和文化背景的要求更大; 2. 阅读、写作部分非常吃力,因为学生没有真正经历或者适应中国的情况; 3. 汉字、词汇学习是一方面,另一方面准确理解及在适当的情景运用更不容易; 4. 汉字的笔画及笔顺对于学生来说很难,涉及复杂的句式或话题时更会加深理解的难度; 5. 没有语言环境,得不到锻炼,但是比非汉语专业学生好很多,阅读、写作相对好一些,因为没有语境条件,学习时间不充足,没有一定的目标语言学习环境支持; 6. 文化或者深层次表达很难掌握; 7. 课时少,因为他们每周只有两次课,3个小时; 8. 因为是两种不同语系的语言; 9. 掌握课本内容和具备实际交际能力是两码事; 10. 这需要学生具有一定的基础知识储备,具备较为成熟的学习态度,能正确面对学习中遇到的挫折和困难,还需要有充足的时间来进行大量的汉字和词汇学习

续表

难易度	人数（占比）	原因
有点难/不太容易	11（12.94%）	1. 首先教材上的内容涉及有限,学生的语法需要一直学习,如果不自主学习,很少有时间和环境去交际; 2. 需要语言环境; 3. 汉字的读写对学生来说较难,想要很好地完成不太容易; 4. 因为语法点更加复杂了
不太难/还行	6（7.06%）	因人而异,努力花时间精力的话还是能够做到的
容易	2（2.35%）	5级具备日常常用语
空白/不完整	30（35.29%）	

表4.6显示了教师受试对《等级标准》描述语能不能反映具备5级汉语水平学习者应达到的写作能力要求的判断。大约有68%的教师受试认为描述语可以体现学习者应该达到的要求,但就汉语国际教育实际情况而言,学生要达到上述能力有一定难度;2.35%的教师受试认为此描述语对学习者的要求过于理想化;另有26位的受试未作答。

表4.6　5级写作能力标准教师问卷数据(第12题)($n=85$)

	人数（占比）	原因
能	39(45.88%)	整体较好,无补充
基本可以	18(21.18%)	能反映,但是难度过高;大多数中级学生水平达不到这么高。因为学习对象年龄结构不同,对于学习知识点和文化因素理解也不同。再者实践活动很难考察,5级学生还需要具备一定的词语辨析能力
不能	2(2.35%)	要求还是过于理想化了,尤其是对于汉字和书面语的习得还是很有限的,写作更难
空白	26(30.59%)	

5 结 论

基于代表性目标受众、通过大规模问卷调查进行的效度验证本质上是"数据驱动(data-driven)"的。本研究中的事前效度验证尚需但不限于以下研究的交叉验证：(1) 更多理论探索；(2) 教师、专家、教育管理者、政策制定者等更广泛利益相关者视角；(3) 分母语语种、分区域的事后效度证据，以及环境效度、效标关联效度证据和反拨效应证据；(4)《等级标准》与考试的关系研究；(5) 研究方法上补充深度访谈、眼动等数据；(6) 与有关考试的对接研究(Kolen et al.，2004；何莲珍，2019)。

效度验证在教育测量及其标准制定中具有举足轻重的地位，是《等级标准》面向全球发布、实施、应用的有力支撑。本研究中全球代表性学生受众的反馈数据表明，《等级标准》5级写作能力描述语的有效性较好，总体效度较理想，与《等级标准》理论构念匹配度较高，语言量化指标反映了中文的语言特点，在国际语言能力标准中独树一帜，体现了中国智慧。

本研究进程中也发现了如下需从多方面考虑的问题：《等级标准》5级描述语对象似偏重成人，建议适当考虑学习者年龄、学段、汉语作为外语的特点等因素对《等级标准》进行改写，突出汉字书写要求，适当降低对低龄学习者不太适合的写作能力要求。

此外，《等级标准》发布实施后，有必要对其进行动态、持续性的事后效度验证。可参照测试使用论证框架(Bachman et al.，2010)对研发者期待的后果效度从以下方面进行研究：(1) 根据具体情境，明确研发和应用《等级标准》的目标效果是什么，哪些利益相关人将从中受益，基于《等级标准》的可能决策有哪些。(2) 如何保证使用《等级标准》后，不同利益相关群体均从中受益？(3) 如何保证《等级标准》落地后，全球不同区块依其所作的决策对所有受影响的利益相关人都有益？(4) 设若有《等级标准》有不准确之处，将产生什么有害后果？如何降低其影响？再版应注意什么问题？上述研究将有利促进《等级标准》以更公平、公正、公开、科学的方式在全球落地。

参考文献：

方绪军，杨惠中，2017. 语言能力等级量表的效度及效度验证[J]. 外国语（上海外国语大学学报），40(4)：2-14.

何莲珍，2019. 语言考试与语言标准对接的效度验证框架[J]. 现代外语，42(5)：660-671.

刘建达，彭川，2017. 构建科学的中国英语能力等级量表[J]. 外语界 (2)：2-9.

刘利，2021. 服务新时代语言学的新发展[J]. 世界汉语教学，35(4)：435-437.

刘英林，李佩泽，李亚男，2020. 汉语国际教育汉语水平等级标准全球化之路[J]. 世界汉语教学，34(2)：147-157.

曾用强，2020. 职业英语能力构念的实证研究[J]. 外语界 (2)：12-19.

中华人民共和国教育部，国家语言文字工作委员会. 国际中文教育中文水平等级标准：GF 0025—2021[S/OL]. (2021-03-24)[2021-08-10]. http://www.moe.gov.cn/jyb_xwfb/gzdt_gzdt/s5987/202103/W020210329527301787356.pdf.

AERA, APA, NCME, 2014. Standards for educational and psychological testing[M]. Washington, DC: American Educational Research Association.

Alderson J C, 2007. The CEFR and the need for more research[J]. The modern language journal, 91(4): 659-663.

Bachman L F, Palmer A S, 2010. Language assessment in practice: developing language assessments and justifying their use in the real world[M]. Oxford: Oxford University Press.

Berger A, 2020. Specifying progression in academic speaking: A keyword analysis of CEFR-based proficiency descriptors[J]. Language assessment quarterly, 17(1): 85-99.

Cronbach L J, 1998. Five perspectives on validity argument[M]//Wainer H, Braun H. Test validity. Hillsdale, NJ: Lawrence Erlbaum Associates: 3-17.

Geranpayeh A, Taylor L, 2013. Examining listening: Research and practice in assessing second language listening[M]. Studies in language Testing: Volume 35. Cambridge: Cambridge University Press.

Kane M T, 1992. An argument-based approach to validity[J]. Psychological

Bulletin, 112(3): 527-535.

Khalifa H, Weir C, 2009. Examining reading: Research and practice in assessing second language reading[M]. Studies in language testing: Volume 29, Cambridge: Cambridge University Press.

Kolen M J, Brennan R L, 2004. Test equating, scaling, and linking: Methods and practices[M]. 2nd ed. Berlin: Springer.

Kunnan A J, Milanovic M, 2000. Fairness and validation in language assessment[M]. Oxford, UK: Oxford University Press.

Messicks, 1989. Validity[M]//Linn R L. Educational measurement. 3rd ed. New York, NY: American Council on Education and Macmillan: 13-103.

Piccardo E, North B, 2020. The dynamic nature of plurilingualism: Creating and validating CEFR descriptors for mediation, plurilingualism and pluricultural competence[M]//Lau S M C, Viegen S V. Plurilingual pedagogies. Cham: Springer: 279-301.

Shaw S, Weir C, 2007. Examining writing: Research and practice in assessing second language writing[M]. Studies in language testing: Volume 26, Cambridge: Cambridge University Press.

Taylor L, 2011. Examining Speaking: Research and practice in assessing second language speaking[M]. Studies in language testing: Volume 30. Cambridge: Cambridge University Press.

Weir C J, 2005. Language testing and validation: An evidence-based approach [M]. Basingstoke: Palgrave Macmillan.

Wisniewski K, 2018. The empirical validity of the common European framework of reference scales: An exemplary study for the vocabulary and fluency scales in a language testing context[J]. Applied linguistics, 39(6): 933-959.

第二部分

Aligning HSK Level 5 Writing Test with *Chinese Proficiency Grading Standards for International Chinese Language Education*
(HSK5写作能力与《国际中文教育中文水平等级标准》的对接研究)

6 Introduction

This chapter covers three sections. It will first introduce the research background of this study, followed by research objectives. Then, the research significance will be elaborated.

6.1 Research Background

Both tests and language standards are measuring instruments. Tests are designed to collect information for evaluation (Bachman, 1990). Language standards, also called language scales, provide a series of descriptors which are statements describing the level of performance required of test takers at each point on the language standards (Han, 2006; Davies et al., 2002). For example, *Common European Framework of Reference for Languages: Learning, Teaching, Assessment* (CEFR) published by the Council of Europe in 2001 is the most influential language standard in the world. On the basis of *CEFR*, many countries have developed their language standards and refined their assessment systems. For instance, *China's Standards of English Language Ability* (CSE) was released in 2018.

Scores of a test can be meaningful when they are put in a reference system. Without a language standard, users of test scores, along with test takers themselves can only possibly analyze test scores by making comparisons among scores (Zhou, 2020). Therefore, it is of great significance to make a connection or an alignment between test scores and language standards.

Aligning tests with language standards is usually considered the process of establishing cut-off scores (Council of Europe, 2009). The minimum test scores required for each level of language standards are referred to as cut-off scores (Papageorgiou et al., 2015). For example, a numerical score of 10 or more on the test leads to Level 3 or a higher performance level of language standards, while a lower score leads to a performance level lower than Level 3. In this sense, linking tests to language standards is a commonly used way of interpreting test scores.

To provide guidance for aligning studies, the Council of Europe (2009) released *Relating Language Examinations to the Common European Framework of Reference for Languages: Learning, Teaching, Assessment (CEFR): A Manual* (hereinafter, the *Manual*) in which steps and methods of aligning tests with language standards have been introduced in detail. Most aligning studies took the *Manual* as a reference. However, Tannenbaum et al. (2014) pointed out that not all studies followed the guidelines or followed them to the same extent, which indicated the complexity and flexibility of aligning studies.

As introduced in the *Manual*, there are four steps of aligning: familiarization, specification, standard setting, and validation (Council of Europe, 2009). Familiarization is the preparational step requiring all participants involved to have a detailed knowledge of language standards. Specification refers to the process of exploring the extent to which tests can be related to language standards from the content perspective, or the process of content alignment (Papageorgiou et al., 2019; Papageorgiou et al., 2015). In the step of standard setting, a decision is usually made to allocate examinees to one of the scale levels based on their performance on the test (Council of Europe, 2009; Green, 2018). The decision is usually made on cut-off scores of examinees' borderline performance (Council of Europe, 2009; Hidri, 2021). Since a satisfactory content alignment is the premise of standard setting (Papageorgiou et al., 2015; Green, 2018; He, 2019), it's necessary to explore whether tests adequately cover the language activities described in language standards before setting cut-off scores to differentiate learners' proficiency levels. Validation is a process of collecting evidence of validity, and should be continuously focused on during the whole process of aligning.

Research on aligning tests with language standards is in full swing abroad, but still in the budding phase at home. During the past years, researchers have aligned many international and local English language tests with *CEFR*. Although *CEFR* is Europe-oriented and based on languages in Europe (Zhang etal., 2019), Chinese language tests have also been aligned with it because of the lack of a Chinese-centered language standard. For example, as an international standardized Chinese language proficiency test, Hanyu Shuiping Kaoshi (HSK) or Chinese proficiency test is designed to assess the communicative ability of non-native speakers of Chinese in their life and work (Zhang et al., 2010; Hanban, 2015), has been aligned with *CEFR* (Xie, 2011).

Aligning Chinese language tests with *CEFR* contributes to the promotion and globalization of Chinese language tests, but it also indicates that international Chinese language education has been following the pace of Western language education for a long time. It is urgent to supply the lack of research on aligning Chinese language tests with Chinese-centered language standards.

Liu et al. (2020) mentioned that the development and reform of Chinese language standards has undergone 4 stages. In 1988, the first version of Chinese language standard was published, but it only described learners' performance of Level 3. Then in 1996, descriptions of learners' performance of Level 4 and Level 5 were covered in the second version of Chinese language standard. There exists no research on aligning Chinese language tests with Chinese language standards until the year 2009. Zhang et al. (2009) tried to relate HSK to *Chinese Language Proficiency Scales for Speakers of Other Languages* (CLPS) released in 2007. CLPS is the third version of Chinese language standard. However, the past decades witnessed significant changes in society, which resulted in great changes in international Chinese language education, calling for an up-to-date or the fourth version of Chinese language standard.

Chinese Proficiency Grading Standards for International Chinese Language Education (hereinafter, the *Standards*) newly formulated echo today's challenges in the field of international Chinese language education (Liu et al., 2020). It's an official Chinese-centered language standard, and has aroused worldwide attention (Li, 2021). Aligning Chinese language tests with the *Standards* should be put on the agenda as soon as possible.

6.2 Research Objectives

HSK is crucial for foreigners who intend to study Chinese, pursue academic degrees in China, and engage in exchanges and cooperation with China (Liu, 1989; Liu, 1994; Zhao, 2016). It consists of 6 levels. Compared with other levels of HSK tests, HSK Level 5 has the largest number of test takers (Fu et al., 2013), because it is normally considered the Chinese language threshold of degree studies in institutes of higher learning and job market in China (Zhang et al., 2021). HSK Level 5 aims at evaluating learners' ability to use Chinese from three dimensions: listening comprehension, reading comprehension and written expression, which explains the reasons why HSK Level 5 includes listening, reading and writing subtests (Hanban, 2015; Fu et al., 2013).

Compared with the listening and reading subtests in the form of multiple-choice items, HSK writing subtests are relatively suitable for the evaluation of examinees' communicative language ability. As introduced by Hanban (2015), HSK Level 5 writing test can be divided into two sections. Section One contains 8 tasks, and each task provides a few words from a sentence in a disordered order. Examinees are requested to put the given words in order logically and then complete sentences. Section Two includes 2 tasks requiring test takers to write a short passage of 80 Chinese characters according to several words or a picture provided. Although the quality of HSK Level 5 is guaranteed, the quality of tasks in Section One of the writing test remains a problem (Fu et al., 2013). Therefore, the present study only focuses on the two tasks in Section Two of HSK Level 5 writing test. These two tasks are Item 99 and Item 100 of HSK Level 5.

In conclusion, considering the urgency of aligning Chinese language tests with Chinese-centered language standards, this study aims at relating HSK Level 5 writing test with the *Standards*, with a particular focus on Items 99 and 100.

6.3 Research Significance

As a preliminary attempt, this study aims at aligning HSK with the *Standards* published in 2021. Although it can only shed light on a small tip of the iceberg, it's hoped that it could serve as a trial or a reference for future aligning studies. The significance of this research is unveiled from four aspects as follows.

Firstly, aligning research is still in its infancy, especially in China. Most aligning studies try to align international and local English language tests, such as International English Language Testing System (IELTS), Test of English as a Foreign Language (TOEFL), College English Test (CET), and Test for English Major (TEM), with *CEFR* or *CSE*. Chinese language tests have also been aligned with *CEFR* which is a Europe-oriented language standard. The *Standards* formulated in 2021 is a Chinese-centered language standard. Aligning HSK, a Chinese language test, with the *Standards* contributes to improving the influence and globalization of Chinese language, as well as promoting the development of International Chinese language education.

Secondly, in terms of aligning steps and methods, the present study is innovative and enlightening. Different from most aligning studies, this study highlights both specification and standard-setting steps, based on the aligning methods introduced in the *Manual* published by the Council of Europe in 2009. Specifically, both quantitative and qualitative methods are used to align HSK with the *Standards* from the content perspective. As for the step of standard setting, both HSK test takers and experts are participants.

Thirdly, the findings of this study are beneficial for the refinement of the *Standards* and the reform of HSK. During a reasonable process of developing a test, publishing a language standard should be followed by designing a test (Zhang et al., 2009). In other words, tests are usually based on standards. Besides, the aim of aligning tests with language standards is interpreting test results based on the standards, which indicates the great importance of the validity of tests.

Fourthly, by providing a more transparent interpretation of HSK scores, this study plays a significant role in promoting the adjustment of international Chinese language education system and the orderly connection among language learning, teaching and testing. To be specific, it will be much easier for Chinese learners to know their actual Chinese proficiency. Chinese language teachers will have a clear grasp of students' Chinese abilities. And for policy makers who set language proficiency requirements, they can have a better understanding of scores and results of HSK tests, and formulate more reasonable policies.

7 Literature Review

This chapter can be divided into five sections. Firstly, definitions, steps, and methods of aligning, as well as the research on aligning English and Chinese language tests with language standards will be covered. Secondly, the research on the *Standards* will be introduced from five aspects, including the development and reform of Chinese language standards, the comparison between Chinese language standards and other language standards, theoretical grounding of the *Standards*, as well as the conceptual framework of the *Standards*. Besides, similar to other language standards, the *Standards* can also be divided into several sub-scales in terms of different language skills, such as listening sub-scales, reading sub-scales, speaking sub-scales, and writing sub-scales (Center for Language Education and Cooperation, 2021a). Thus, considering the objectives of the present study, the writing sub-scales of the *Standards* will be mentioned in this section as well. Thirdly, previous research on HSK will be presented from three perspectives, including the development and reform of HSK, the construct of HSK, and HSK Level 5. Fourthly, four research questions will be presented. In the end, a summary of this chapter will be given.

7.1 Aligning Tests with Language Standards

First, definitions of aligning will be given. Then, four steps of aligning will be explained. In the end, relevant studies of aligning English language tests and Chinese language tests with language standards will be presented.

7.1.1 Definitions of Aligning

In general, aligning is the process of linking two independent measuring instruments like tests to tests, language standards to language standards, and tests to language standards (He et al., 2020). Both tests and language standards are measuring instruments. But various tests and standards are different in contents, ways and the difficulty of measuring (Kolen et al., 2004). Tests are designed to collect information for evaluation (Bachman, 1990). Language standards provide a series of descriptors which are the statements describing the level of performance required of test takers at each point on the language proficiency standards (Han, 2006; Davies et al., 2002).

Traditionally, aligning refers to the process of linking the results of tests and finding the extent to which tests can be equivalent (Lu, 2011a). In other words, aligning refers to equating. It means that, for example, a score of 450 on College English Test Band 4 is largely equivalent in meaning to a score of 6 on International English Language Testing System (IELTS). The objective of equating is to get interchangeable scores (Newton, 2010). However, what is noteworthy is that tests are designed for different groups of people with various purposes, which suggests the infeasibility of the equivalence of scores from different tests. Thus, when comparing two tests, researchers should pay attention to not only the equivalence of test results, but also the contents of tests and candidates' performance (Bachman, 1995). Aligning tests with a single language standard is used to make the comparison between tests. For example, Chen and Hu (2020) linked IELTS and APTIS to the same language standard. The results of their study contribute to making the results of those two tests comparable on different occasions and building a mutual recognition between the two tests.

The alignment between two language standards equals to the correspondence between them (Lee, 2018; Peng et al., 2021). In the field of language testing, standards and scales can be used interchangeably. Among language standards or scales around the world, *CEFR* is the most influential one. It allocates language learners to six language proficiency levels. During the past decades, most researchers have focused on aligning other language standards with *CEFR*. In China, *CSE* is a representative language standard or scale, and it allocates English learners to 9 levels according to their English proficiency. Since its release, *CSE* has aroused researchers' interest. And researchers have tried to link *CSE* to *CEFR*.

Research on aligning *CSE* with *CEFR* can be generally divided into two groups: the alignment between overall language proficiency scales, and the alignment between sub-scales. Peng et al. (2021) focused on the overall language proficiency scales, and made a level alignment between *CSE* and *CEFR*, because both *CEFR* and *CSE* can be further divided into several sub-scales according to different language skills, such as writing sub-scales, listening sub-scales, reading sub-scales and so on. Therefore, many aligning studies lay emphasis on sub-scales. For example, Peng et al. (2021) related levels of *CEFR* to those of *CSE*, with a focus on writing sub-scales, through a questionnaire survey. Besides, Peng et al. also explored the level alignment between *CEFR* and *CSE* in terms of listening sub-scales.

As for the definition of aligning tests with language standards, the foremost should be the distinction between content standards and performance standards. Content standards indicate the alignment from the perspective of content or the content alignment. As explained by Hambleton (2001), content standards refer to the curriculum, as well as what test takers are expected to know and to be able to do. In this sense, content alignment can refer to the process of exploring the extent to which the test content can cover the skills or abilities described in language standards (Papageorgiou et al., 2019).

Performance standards refer to the level of performance that is expected of test takers to demonstrate, say, Basic, Proficient, and Advanced level performance in relation to the content standards (Hambleton, 2001). In this sense, performance standards focus on the degree to which test takers are expected to perform in relation to the content standards. The Council of Europe (2009) has also mentioned that "a performance standard is the boundary between two levels on the continuum scale reported by a test that is represented by a cut-off score". In other words, a performance standard is usually expressed as the cut-off score (Green, 2018). Therefore, aligning tests with language standards is usually regarded as the process of establishing cut-off scores (Council of Europe, 2009), setting performance standards (Green, 2018), allocating learners to different levels of performance, or mapping test scores with levels of language standards. Cut-off scores present the minimum test scores required for each level of language standards or scales (Papageorgiou et al., 2015). For example, a numerical score of 10 or more on the test leads to Level 3 or a higher proficiency level in a language standard, while a lower score leads to a level lower than Level 3.

In terms of the relationship between making content alignment and setting performance standards, satisfactory content alignment is the premise of setting performance standards (Papageorgiou et al., 2015; Green, 2017). Therefore, it's necessary to make the content alignment between tests and language standards first.

7.1.2 Steps and Methods of Aligning Tests with Language Standards

Most studies of aligning tests with language standards take the *Manual* as a reference. Hence, in this section, aligning steps introduced in the *Manual* will be presented in detail.

In order to achieve greater unity and promote cooperation among its members, the Council of Europe realized the importance of languages and communication, as well as the urgency of establishing a common language proficiency standard. Then *CEFR* was released in 2001.

CEFR is the most influential language standard around the world. On the basis of *CEFR*, many countries around the world have developed their language standards, and refined their assessment system. For example, *CSE* was released in 2018.

CEFR provides a basis for developing and describing language syllabuses, curriculum guidelines, tests, textbooks and so on across Europe. It comprehensively describes "what language learners have to learn to do in order to use a language for communication and what knowledge and skills they have to develop so as to be able to act effectively" (Council of Europe, 2001). *CEFR* also describes different levels of language proficiency, which ensures the possibility of measuring learners' progress in language learning. Specifically, according to learners' language proficiency, *CEFR* allocates learners to six levels which are Breakthrough (A1), Waystage (A2), Threshold (B1), Vantage (B2), Effective Operational Proficiency (C1) and Mastery (C2) (Council of Europe, 2001).

In 2009, the Council of Europe released the *Manual* to provide a scientific alignment system and procedure for aligning tests with *CEFR*, which helps to deal with bias and improve the validity of aligning. As is introduced in the *Manual*, there are four steps in the process of aligning: familiarization, specification, standard setting and validation (Council of Europe, 2009).

Familiarization is the preparational step before the step of both specification and standard setting, and it requires all participants involved to have a detailed knowledge of the language standard, including its levels and descriptors (Council of Europe, 2009).

Specification and standard setting are the essential steps of the whole aligning process. The end product of specification is a claim about the content alignment, as well as a description of the examination in relation to *CEFR* categories and levels (Council of Europe, 2009). The Council of Europe also mentioned that a decision is usually made in the step of standard setting to allocate learners to one of the scale levels based on their performance on the test, and the decision is usually made on cut-off scores of examinees' borderline performance.

Specification is the process of making the content alignment, while standard setting serves as the process of setting performance standards (Green, 2018). If the degree of content alignment is unsatisfactory, there will be no significance in aligning studies (He, 2019). In other words, content alignment is the premise of aligning studies.

Specification is also considered as the process of collecting construct validity. As mentioned in *Standards for Educational Psychological Testing*, "validity refers to the degree to which evidence and theory support the interpretations of test scores for proposed uses of tests" (American Educational Research Association et al.,

2005). American Educational Research Association et al. also mentioned that the evidence for validity can be gathered from an analysis of the relation between the test content and the construct of the test, which is normally called the process of collecting evidence for the construct validity. Construct here refers to what a test aims to assess (Bachman, 1990).

Standard setting is the process of setting performance standards (Green, 2018). There are two kinds of standard-setting methods, test-centered and examinee-centered methods (Jaeger, 1989; Kaftandjieva, 2004). Test-centered methods include the Tucker-Angoff, Yes-No, extended Tucker-Angoff, item-descriptor matching, and basket methods (Council of Europe, 2009). Their focus is not the actual performance of examinees, but the test papers which reflect the expected performance of examinees (Bechger et al., 2009). The contrasting groups, borderline group, and body of work are examinee-centered methods (Council of Europe, 2009). Those methods require examinees' actual performance (Bechger et al., 2009). Therefore, test-centered methods are suitable for aligning tests of receptive language skills with language standards, while examinee-centered methods are usually used to align tests of productive language skills with language standards (Kane, 1998).

Validation is a process of collecting evidence of validity and should be continuously focused on during the whole process of aligning. Evidence of procedural, external and internal validity will be collected (Council of Europe, 2009).

Procedural validity means that each step of aligning research should be implemented validly. Evidence, such as judges' familiarity with the scales, their understanding of aligning methods, and their confidence in the actual operation of the aligning is usually collected by questionnaires to ensure procedural validity (Council of Europe, 2009).

Internal validity highlights the accuracy and consistency of aligning results. Only if it is ensured that the way of using, applying and interpreting the *CEFR* descriptors is shared and agreed upon by judges who match test tasks or test takers' performance with a specific level of the language standard can the aligning results be valid (Council of Europe, 2009). It explains the necessity of the step of familiarization, and the importance of inter-rater consistency and intra-rater consistency (Harsch et al., 2020). Therefore, before aligning candidates' performance or test tasks with language standards' levels, participants should have a training session, so as to reach a consensus on the understanding of the descriptors in the specific language standard (Council of Europe, 2009; Cizek, 2001).

External validity concerns about the generalization of aligning results. Any factor that makes aligning results limited in a specific condition will bring damage to the external validity. As introduced in the *Manual*, results of an aligning study are affected by the procedure carried out by the same person or the same group of persons, as well as influenced by the test data collected in a single condition (Council of Europe, 2009). Therefore, factors affecting the external validity include the characteristics of participants, research procedure and so on.

Although aligning steps and methods covered in the *Manual* have been considered as guidelines, and used widely around the world, Tannenbaum et al. (2014) pointed out that not all aligning studies follow the guidelines or follow them to the same extent, which suggests the complexity and flexibility of aligning studies. In the following sections, studies of aligning tests with language standards, especially aligning procedures and methods used in the studies, will be presented.

7.1.3 Aligning English Language Tests with Language Standards

Since the release of *CEFR* in 2001, Chinese researchers have tried to use *CEFR* innovatively in China, such as developing a common English proficiency standard for China's English learners, revising Chinese proficiency standards and so on (Zou et al., 2015). In 2018, *CSE* was released by the Ministry of Education of the People's Republic of China and the National Language Commission of the People's Republic of China. Therefore, in this section, research on aligning English language tests with language standards, such as *CEFR* and *CSE*, will be covered. Table 7.1 lists the main aligning studies.

In terms of the steps of aligning, most studies follow the steps recommended by the *Manual*. And they not only make content alignment, but

Table 7.1 Studies on Aligning English Language Tests with Language Standards

Studies	Tests	Standards	Methods of Content Alignment	Methods of Setting Performance Standards
Tannenbaum & Wylie (2008)	TOEFL® iBT test, TOEIC® assessment, TOEIC Bridge™ test	CEFR	Not introduced	Modified Angoff method, modified examinee paper selection method
Huang & Jia (2012)	CET	CEFR	Qualitative research method	Not mentioned
Wang (2015)	TEM	CEFR	Qualitative research method	Not mentioned
Fleckenstein et al. (2019)	TOEFL®4 iBT writing test	CEFR	Qualitative research method	Modified examinee paper selection/performance profile method
Dunlea et al. (2019)	Aptis, IELTS	CSE	Qualitative research method	Basket method, modified Angoff method, contrasting group method
Papageorgiou et al. (2019)	TOEFL iBT®	CSE	Qualitative research method	Modified Angoff method, modified performance profile/examinee paper selection method
Harsch & Kanistra (2020)	The Trinity College London (TCL) Integrated Skills of English ISE writing exams	CEFR	Not introduced	Item-descriptor matching method, benchmarking approach
Zhou (2020)	Reading tests of NMET	CSE	Qualitative research method	Basket method, modified Angoff method
Min & Jiang (2020)	Listening tests of an in-house English proficiency test	CSE	Qualitative research method	Modified Angoff method, contrasting group method
Wang (2020)	Shanghai Jiao Tong University English Proficiency Test	CSE	Not introduced	A student-centered research method

also set performance standards. However, some studies only focus on content alignment which suggests the feasibility of aligning studies (Huang et al., 2012; Wang, 2015).

Content alignment is usually addressed by judges to make a qualitative evaluation of tests in relation to language standards from the content perspective (Council of Europe, 2009). Materials related to the development of tests, such as curriculum syllabus, sample test papers, teaching syllabus and test syllabus, can reflect the construct of tests. Making a comparison between those materials and language standards is a commonly used method of making content alignment.

For example, Hang et al. (2012) discussed the feasibility of linking CET to *CEFR* by relating *College English Curriculum Requirements* and CET sample test papers with *CEFR* from the content perspective. Besides, Wang (2015) explored the feasibility of aligning TEM with *CEFR* by making a content analysis of sample test papers, teaching syllabi, and test syllabi in relation to *CEFR*. Papageorgiou et al. (2019) made content alignment by reviewing materials related to the design of the test, and those materials were presented on the official website. In addition, Khalifa et al. (2009) also mentioned that materials specifying the construct of the test and explaining how the test was implemented effectively, such as the guidelines for item writers, and scoring manuals, should be analyzed when mapping the content of the test onto the language standards.

However, content alignment is always made by a qualitative research method, and the number of participants is limited. Thus, given those limitations, the present study uses a combination of both qualitative and quantitative methods. To be specific, a qualitative content analysis of HSK Rating Criteria, *HSK Test Syllabus* and *HSK Test Item-writing Manual* will be made. Besides, experts will be invited to complete a questionnaire and make the judgment on the relation between HSK sample test papers and the *Standards* from the content perspective.

Setting performance standards aims at mapping test scores on levels of language standards. It focuses on examinees' performance on tests, and is usually made by test-centered or examinee-centered methods. Test-centered methods, such as modified Angoff method (Tannenbaum et al., 2008; Dunlea et al., 2019; Papageorgiou et al., 2019; Zhou, 2020; Min et al., 2020), basket method (Dunlea et al., 2019; Zhou, 2019), and item-descriptor matching methods (Harsch et al., 2020), are usually used to align tests of receptive language skills with language standards. Examinee-centered methods, such as the examinee paper selection method (Tannenbaum et al., 2008; Fleckenstein et al., 2019; Papageorgiou et al., 2019), the contrasting group method (Dunlea et al., 2019; Min et al., 2020), and the benchmarking method (Harsch et al., 2020), are usually used to align tests of productive language skills with language standards. However, Harsch et al. (2020) combined the test-centered method with the examinee-centered method to align writing tests with *CEFR*, which suggests an innovative standard-setting method. Besides, Min et al. (2020) also took a combined method to align listening tests with *CEFR*.

Instead of using test-centered or examinee-centered standard-setting methods, Wang (2020) took a student-centered method to align Shanghai Jiao Tong University English Proficiency Test (SJTU-EPT) with *CSE*. The aligning judgment is usually made by experts or teachers. But in Wang's study, both teachers and students made the judgment. Specifically, Wang designed questionnaires to collect students' self-evaluation of their language ability, and teachers' evaluation of those students' language ability. Students needed to evaluate the degree to which they could reach the requirements of *CSE* Levels 4 to 7. Teachers who were familiar with those students' actual language ability tried to allocate students to different levels of *CSE*. Combining the results of both students' self-evaluation and teachers' judgment, Wang concluded that the seven reported levels of SJTU-EPT can be linked to *CSE* Levels 4 to 8.

To sum up, when setting performance standards, most aligning studies use either test-centered methods or examinee-centered methods. When aligning tests of productive language skills with language standards, examinee-centered methods are usually adopted. However, considering the innovative methods presented by Wang (2020), the present study will use a combination of both examinee-centered and student-centered methods. Specifically, HSK Level 5 examinees will evaluate their writing ability. Meanwhile, experts will be invited to make the judgment on examinees' written scripts in relation to the *Standards*. Thus, the performance standards will be set on the basis of both examinees' self-evaluation and experts' judgment.

In terms of the validation, evidence of procedural validity, internal validity and external validity are not always reported at the same time. Some studies report evidence of two of them. For example, Tannenbaum et al. (2008) provided positive evidence of procedural and external validity. Harsch et al. (2020) reported inter-rater consistency and intra-rater consistency, which could reflect the internal validity of aligning results. They also designed questionnaires to collect data for procedural validity. Fleckenstein et al. (2019) discussed the internal and procedural validity. Some studies only discuss the external validity. For example, Zhou (2020) and Wang (2020) discussed the external validity by exploring the correlations among test scores, teachers' assessments and students' self-assessments.

Therefore, to ensure the validity of the present study, the correlations between HSK scores and examinees' self-evaluation, and between HSK scores and experts' judgment, will be analyzed.

7.1.4 Aligning Chinese Language Tests with Language Standards

Many Chinese language tests have also been aligned with *CEFR*. Lu (2011a) explored the linkage between the reading sections of Business Chinese Test (BCT) and *CEFR* from the content perspective. Lu (2011b) also analyzed the relation between BCT and *CEFR* by following the steps of standard setting mentioned in the *Manual*.

What is noteworthy is that Luo (2017) did not follow the whole steps mentioned in the *Manual*. Based on the test scores, students' self-assessment data, and teachers' evaluation, Luo's study discussed the relation between a Chinese placement test and *CEFR*, and she also pointed out the crucial role that the validity of research instruments played. Ensuring the validity of research instruments is beneficial to ensure the validity of the aligning study. Thus, the quality of research instruments will also be considered in the present study.

After the release of *CEFR*, *Chinese Language Proficiency Scales for Speakers of Other Languages* (*CLPS*) were promulgated in 2007. Zhang et al. (2009) tried to relate HSK to *CLPS*. Similar to Wang (2020) and Luo (2017), Zhang et al. invited both examinees and teachers as participants or judges, and the aligning results were based on both examinees' self-evaluation and teachers' judgment. First of all, they invited experts to link HSK scores to *CLPS*. Then experts' judgment was verified in a quantitative method. To be specific, researchers organized Chinese language learners of targeted proficiency levels to take HSK tests, and then obtained HSK scores of those learners. At the same time, they invited the Chinese teachers of those learners to classify those learners into *CLPS* levels because those teachers had an comparatively objective and accurate grasp of those learners' Chinese language proficiency. Besides, those Chinese teachers also made the judgment on the abilities and skills which level of *CLPS* was required to answer the test items correctly. In the end, a brief connection between HSK and *CLPS* was reported.

In conclusion, there are limited studies of aligning Chinese language tests with Chinese language standards. The aligning methods introduced by Wang (2020), Luo (2017) and Zhang et al. (2009) are enlightening for the present study. Thus, both HSK Level 5 examinees and experts will be invited as participants or judges of the present study, so as to make the aligning results more reliable.

7.2 *Chinese Proficiency Grading Standards for International Chinese Language Education*

As the latest version of the Chinese language standard, *Chinese Proficiency Grading Standards for International Chinese Language Education* was released in 2021. The development and reform of Chinese language standards, as well as the comparison between Chinese language standards and other language standards will be introduced in this section.

It has already been explained in Section 7.1 that making content alignment is necessary for an aligning study. To have a satisfactory degree of content alignment, the construct of tests and that of language standards should share a great number of characteristics. Construct refers to what a test or language standard aims to assess. Therefore, the theoretical grounding and conceptual framework of the *Standards* will be provided. Since the present study only focuses on the HSK Level 5 writing test, the writing sub-scales of the *Standards* will be further explained.

In conclusion, this chapter introduces relevant research from the following aspects: (1) the development and reform of Chinese language standards; (2) the comparison between Chinese language standards and other language standards; (3) the theoretical grounding of the *Standards*; (4) the conceptual framework of the *Standards*; and (5) the writing sub-scales of the *Standards*.

7.2.1 The Development and Reform of Chinese Language Standards

In the 1990s, with the acceleration of the European integration process, people realized the importance of language and communication and believed that it was necessary to establish a common language proficiency standard. Therefore, *CEFR* emerged then. Language proficiency standards are used to evaluate learners' language competence, and they usually contain a series of descriptors. Descriptors are the statements describing the level of performance required of test takers at each point on the language proficiency standards or scales (Davies et al., 2002).

With the growing importance of Chinese language in international communication and exchanges, an increasing number of people have begun to learn Chinese. Under this circumstance, there is a need to assess learners' Chinese language ability for various purposes. Tests are usually used for the evaluation (Bachman, 1990). With the increase of large-scale Chinese proficiency tests, it is urgent to make a comparison between those tests and test results, which is the basis for making appropriate decisions (Fang, 2007). The lack of a common reference for making the comparison is the main obstacle. Obviously, a scientific and widely accepted Chinese language standard is of great importance for both Chinese language education and Chinese language testing.

Officially released on March 31, 2021, and implemented on July 1, 2021, *Chinese Proficiency Grading Standards for International Chinese Language Education* defines learners' Chinese communicative proficiency in specific situations such as daily life, study, and workplace (Center for Language Education and Cooperation, 2021a). The *Standards* are globally oriented with distinctive characteristics of the times (Li, 2021).

7.2.2 The Comparison between Chinese Language Standards and Other Language Standards

The main influential language proficiency scales in the world include *Canadian Language Benchmarks* (CLB) (Grazyna, 2000), *Common European Framework of Reference for Languages: Learning, Teaching, Assessment* (CEFR) (Council of Europe, 2001), *Interagency Language Roundtable Scale* (*ILR Scale*) (Interagency Roundtable, 1985), (ACTFL) *Proficiency Guidelines* (American Council on the Teaching of Foreign Languages, 2012) and so on. In China, we have *China's Standards of English Language Ability* (CSE) (National Education Examinations Authority, 2018).

Sheng (1988) made a comparison between the first version of the Chinese proficiency standard published in 1988 and three language proficiency standards in America, with a focus on the level classification. Sheng concluded that although many international and domestic language proficiency standards were based on the theory of communicative language competence, those standards were not systematic due to the lack of further research on language competence and language education.

Cheng (2011) compared the *CLPS* published in 2007 with two well-recognized foreign language proficiency standards which were *CLB* and *CEFR* respectively. Based on Bachman's theory of communicative language competence, Cheng's research focused on linguistic, textual, functional, sociolinguistic and strategic abilities, concluding that similar with *CEFR* and *CSE*, *CLPS* was designed to assess learners' language communicative competence.

Li et al. (2020) analyzed the descriptors in *CSE*, *CEFR*, *CLB*, *ILR Scale*, *(ACTFL) Proficiency Guidelines* and *CLPS* in both quantitative and qualitative ways. According to their quantitative analysis, the quality of *CLPS* was far lower than those of other standards in terms of the average fineness and fineness deviation, which called for an enrichment of the number of descriptors. Besides, listening, reading, speaking and writing skills were core parameters of language standards, which explained the reason why language standards were usually divided into listening, reading, speaking and writing sub-scales. In terms of the results of their qualitative analysis, "can-do" descriptors and affirmative expressions were the mainstream descriptors in most language standards, except *CLB*, *ILR Scale* and *(ACTEL) Proficiency Guidelines*. "Can-do" descriptors indicated that most language standards highlighted learners' communicative language ability, and took the theory of communicative language ability as their theoretical grounding. In this sense, learners' language proficiency could be described as their ability to fulfill communicative tasks in a specific communicative context (Liu, 2015; Liu et al., 2018). Besides, quantitative requirements were rare in most language standards. Li et al. (2020) pointed out that Chinese language was different from Indo-European languages, so quantitative requirements on vocabulary, grammar and Chinese characters should be involved in Chinese language standards.

Zhang (2021) tried to make a comparison between *CEFR* and the *Standards*, but did not make a clear conclusion. Although the relation between the *Standards* and *CEFR* remains a question, some similarities they share can be found in Zhang's study. The descriptors of *CEFR* are stated in the structure of "can-do" and emphasize the communicative function of languages. Numerous foreign language proficiency standards and exams refer to *CEFR* to some extent. For instance, when explaining Chinese language proficiency, HSK tests draw on the internationally popular theory of communicative competence, cover the requirements of "can-do" descriptors, and are directly linked to levels of *CEFR* (Zhang, 2021). Those will undoubtedly contribute to the development of International Chinese language education, the understanding of the whole world on HSK tests, and the internationalization of HSK tests.

In conclusion, most scales in the world are based on the theory of communicative language ability and involve "can-do" descriptors describing learners' ability to fulfill communicative tasks in a specific communicative context. Tests, for example HSK tests, also draw on the theory of communicative language ability. Besides, Chinese language standards should attach much importance to the characteristics of Chinese language and make quantitative requirements on learners' language knowledge of Chinese characters, vocabulary, as well as grammar.

7.2.3 Theoretical Grounding of the *Standards*

After making the comparison among language standards, it can be concluded that cultivating learners' communicative language ability has already been the essential purpose of language education. The theory of communicative language ability has become the basis of developing language standards. Descriptors in language standards are usually stated in the structure of "can-do", which suggests communicative functions of languages. In this sense, learners' language ability is shown by their fulfillment of communicative tasks in a specific context. For example, learners who can do or fulfill tasks mentioned in the descriptors of level 1 can be rated as reaching the level of language proficiency.

The *Standards* define learners' Chinese communicative ability in specific situations such as daily life, study, and workplace (Center for Language Education and Cooperation, 2021a). It also uses "can-do" statements, for example, "can analyze the structure of common Chinese characters". Therefore, its theoretical grounding is the theory of communicative language ability.

However, researchers did not realize the importance of communicative language ability and ignored learners' ability to use language. In this sense, competence first proposed by Chomsky was their interest. Competence refers to one's internal language knowledge, while performance is the actual application of language (Chomsky, 1965). In the view of Chomsky, competence is not related to using language.

Hymes (1972) put forward communicative competence for the first time. He believed that communicative competence was one's ability of listening and speaking and it involved both linguistic competence and the ability to use language. Since then, the communicative competence has aroused researchers' great interest. Then, Canale et al. (1980) divided communicative competence into four chapters: grammatical competence, sociolinguistic competence, strategic competence, and discourse competence.

Bachman (1990) proposed a systematic and comprehensive model called the Model of Communicative Language Ability (CLA). And the communicative language ability was explained as a combination of competence and the capacity to use the competence appropriately. Besides, he also pointed out the interaction among the elements of communicative language ability.

The model of CLA involved three elements: language competence or knowledge, strategic competence, and psychophysiological mechanisms, and a detailed description of the model was explained by Bachman as follows.

Language knowledge consists of two chapters: organizational competence and pragmatic competence. Specifically, organizational competence comprises grammatical competence and textual competence, while pragmatic competence includes sociolinguistic competence and illocutionary competence. Since language is used in a specific context, strategic competence refers to language users' ability to communicate in a specific context. Psychophysiological mechanisms were defined as the psychological and neurological processes in the realistic execution of language in a communicative situation as a physical phenomenon such as sound (Bachman 1990).

In conclusion, the *Standards* are also based on the theory of communicative language ability. According to the model of CLA proposed by Bachman, both language knowledge and learners' ability of using language are highlighted, which explains the reason why the *Standards* focus on learners' verbal communication abilities and make quantitative requirements on learners' language knowledge. The following section will provide a further explanation of the conceptual framework of the *Standards*. Both theoretical grounding and the conceptual framework of the *Standards* reflect the construct of the Standards, which serves as the basis of making content alignment.

7.2.4 The Conceptual Framework of the *Standards*

The conceptual framework of the *Standards* represents not only its theoretical grounding, but also typical characteristics of Chinese language. Analyzing the conceptual framework of the *Standards* is necessary for studies of aligning tests with the *Standards* from the content perspective.

In 2020, an official explanation of the conceptual framework of the *Standards* was provided, and the conceptual framework of the *Standards* presented 3 innovative points or features (Liu et al., 2020). The first innovative point was a total of "three levels and nine bands" which was explained by Liu et al. as follows.

> Chinese proficiency of learners is defined by three levels: the Elementary Level, the Intermediate Level, and the Advanced Level. Within each level, learners' Chinese proficiency is further divided into three bands based on the proficiency difference. (pp.

149-150)

The second aspect was the "3+5" structure of descriptors in each band. A detailed explanation of this aspect was made by Liu et al. as follows.

> The number "3" refers to 3 dimensions of analysis: verbal communication abilities, topics and tasks, and quantitative criteria. The essential purpose of language education and testing is to cultivate learners' communicative language abilities, which is widely accepted in the world. Verbal communication abilities refer to the learners' abilities to use Chinese to communicate on various topics in different contexts. Listening, speaking, reading, writing, and interpreting and translation skills are used comprehensively in communication. Topics are those commonly encountered ones in daily life, study, and workplace. Tasks refer to those typically fulfilled ones. Learners need to use multiple language skills comprehensively to complete those communicative tasks. Quantitative criteria refer to requirements on syllables, Chinese characters, words and phrases, and grammar that learners at each level of Chinese proficiency should master. The number "5" refers to 5 language skills: listening, reading, speaking, writing, translation and interpretation, which corresponds to five sub-scales of the *Standards*. (pp. 150 – 151)

The third category introduced in their study was the four-dimension benchmarks at each band measuring Chinese proficiency based on four basic linguistic elements, including syllables, Chinese characters, words and phrases, and grammar (Liu et al., 2020).

In conclusion, the construct of the *Standards* is learners' ability to use Chinese to communicate in a context to fulfill communicative tasks. Figure 7.1 illustrates the structure of "3 + 5", and four-dimension benchmarks are described as quantitative criteria.

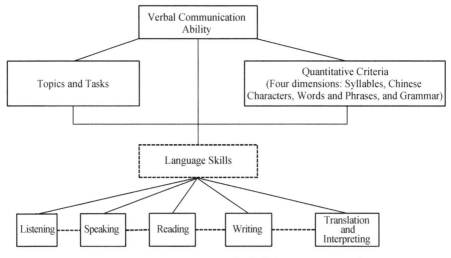

Figure 7.1　The Structure of "3+5" (Liu et al., 2020)

Therefore, the content of the *Standards* can be analyzed from three aspects: (1) the communicative context described as different topics in descriptors; (2) the communicative functions described as communicative tasks in descriptors; and (3) the four-dimensional quantitative criteria representing the importance of Chinese language knowledge in communication. When making content alignment, the content of HSK should be analyzed in relation to the *Standards*. In this sense, the three aspects constitute the framework of the content analysis.

7.2.5　The Writing Sub-scales of the *Standards*

The *Standards* describe learners' communicative language ability in terms of listening comprehension, reading comprehension, oral expression, written expression, and translation and interpretation (Liu et al., 2020). Considering the focus of the present study, the writing sub-scales of the *Standards* will be further introduced.

In the process of developing a writing scale, a reasonable construct of the scale is the theoretical basis and prerequisite, which has become a consensus in the field of language testing (North, 2003). Analyzing the construct of the writing sub-scales in the *Standards* is also the premise of the present study.

The theoretical grounding and conceptual framework of a writing scale reflect its construct. The theoretical grounding describe the construct indirectly, while the conceptual framework of the writing scale reflects the construct directly. According to the theoretical grounding of the *Standards* mentioned before, the construct framework of the writing sub-scales should be in line with CLA. In other words, the construct of the writing sub-scales should be defined from the perspective of CLA.

In order to have a better understanding of the content of the writing sub-scales of the *Standards*, it is necessary to have a close look at the nature and models of writing which serves as the basis of designing a writing scale. Although the description of writing ability has not reached a consensus, and there exists no ready-made theoretical model which can adequately explain writing ability (Knoch, 2009), studies of writing ability generally start from the communicative and cognitive aspects.

Traditional ways of assessing writing are mainly from the cognitive aspects. Various models of the writing process have been put forward. Hayes et al. (1980) first developed a model describing the writing process from the task environment, writers' long-term memory, and a number of cognitive processes. They introduced their model as follows.

> The task environment covers the writing assignment and the text produced. Knowledge of topic, knowledge of audience, and stored writing plans are involved in writers' long-term memory. Cognitive processes mainly include planning, translating thoughts into text, and revising. (pp. 3 – 30)

However, writing is not only a cognitive activity. It should also be considered as a social and cultural phenomenon. Writing is a social act, and it usually happens in a specific social setting. The social setting or the context of writing affects the genre and task of writing. Thus, Hayes (1996) took the social aspects of writing into consideration. And the model put forward by Hayes was described in detail as follows.

> The writing process can be considered as a combination of the

task environment and the individual. Task environment contains the social environment involving the audience and the collaborators, and the physical environment covering text written and composing medium. The individual aspects in the model refer to an interaction among the working memory, motivation and effect, cognitive processes, and long-term memory. The cognitive process involves three elements, text interpretation, reflection and text production. (pp. 1 – 27)

To sum up, Hayes' model only highlights the social aspects of writing. The focus of his model is the individual, rather than the task environment or variables affecting the social setting or context, because Hayes only lists the audience and the collaborators as social factors. In addition to the lack of attention to social aspects of writing, Hayes' model also doesn't attach importance to language knowledge. As mentioned before, writing is not only a social act, but also a cultural act. Cultures have a great influence on many aspects of writing. Grabe et al. (1996) pointed out that different cultures had an ignorable influence on cultural preferences, which further affected the choice of linguistic knowledge. Linguistic knowledge is usually learned through the educational system. Due to the constraints of limited second-language knowledge, second-language writers have to pay much attention to their language, rather than the content of their writing. All those mentioned explain the importance of linguistic knowledge in second-language writing. Thus, the lack of attention to linguistic knowledge in Hayes's model makes it unsuitable to explain the second-language writing ability.

The model proposed by Grabe et al. in 1996 overcomes the limitations of Hayes' model (Weigle, 2002). Grabe et al. proposed a model of writing ability as communicative language use, in which three main elements of writing theory were integrated. The three elements were the writer's cognitive processing, the linguistic and textual resources that constitute writing tasks, and the contextual factors. The model was explained by Grabe et al. as follows.

> The context can be perceived as the external conditions of writing, including the situation or task environment, and the text produced or writers' performance. The situation involves participants, setting, task, text, and topic. The model also presents relevant language knowledge in writing. The language knowledge covers the linguistic, socio-linguistic, and discourse knowledge. (pp. 34 – 57)

According to the theoretical grounding of the *Standards*, the definition of the construct of the writing sub-scales should cover the following aspects: (1) the communicative functions of writing; (2) the communicative context for writing; (3) as well as the language knowledge used in writing.

Besides, it is the quality of learners' performance in writing Chinese characters and writing compositions that the descriptors in the writing sub-scales aim to describe (Center for Language Education and Cooperation, 2021b). Writing is a productive language skill. The quality of learners' writing performance or the produced texts indicates learners' writing ability. In other words, levels of learners' writing ability are judged by the quality of the text they produce.

7.3 Hanyu Shuiping Kaoshi (HSK)

This chapter presents previous research on the Hanyu Shuiping Kaoshi (HSK) or the Chinese Proficiency Test from the following perspectives: (1) the development and reform of HSK; (2) the construct of HSK; and (3) HSK Level 5.

7.3.1 The Development and Reform of HSK

As an international standardized test, HSK is designed to evaluate the ability of non-native speakers of Chinese to communicate in Chinese in their daily life, study and work (Hanban, 2015; Zhang et al., 2010). Similar to IELTS and TOEFL, HSK is a second language or foreign language proficiency test. It is the most influential Chinese proficiency test in the world, and the threshold for foreigners who intend to study Chinese, pursue an academic degree in China, or engage in exchanges and cooperation with China (Liu, 1989; Liu, 1994; Zhao, 2016). But different from IELTS and TOEFL, HSK concentrates on the typical features of Chinese language and shows its uniqueness.

HSK has undergone three stages of development: HSK 1.0, HSK 2.0 and HSK 3.0. HSK 1.0 was developed in 1984, officially implemented in China in the year 1990, and promoted overseas in 1991(Zhang et al., 2010). Liu et al. (1988) reported the reliability and validity of HSK 1.0 and explained its functions and characteristics. Meanwhile, the first version of the Chinese proficiency standard published in 1988 was linked to HSK 1.0. They proposed that HSK 1.0 would take the Chinese proficiency standard as its basis since the year 1988. Actually, during a reasonable process of developing a test, publishing the language proficiency standards should be followed by designing tests (Zhang et al., 2009). However, the first version of the Chinese proficiency standard was released later than HSK 1.0.

In 2009, on the basis of HSK 1.0, the Center for Language Education and Cooperation released the new HSK, namely HSK 2.0. Xie (2011) pointed out four reasons to explain why it was necessary to release HSK 2.0. The first reason was to develop HSK in line with the *CLPS* published in 2007, and the six levels of HSK 2.0 were related to six levels of *CEFR*. The second one was to develop HSK based on the model of communicative language competence. The third one was to lay much emphasis on assessing test takers' spoken and written expression abilities. The last one was to make the structure of HSK more reasonable. Zhang et al. (2010) also introduced the principles of developing HSK 2.0 and the features of HSK 2.0 compared with HSK 1.0. The difficulty of each level of HSK 2.0 was controlled, with vocabulary and question types as important control factors. To be specific, there were six features of HSK 2.0, including expanding the levels of HSK, thinking highly of test takers' ability to apply Chinese, attaching much importance to learners' productive language skills, providing concrete requirements of vocabulary, using more pictures, and marking tasks with Chinese Pinyin.

According to the two studies mentioned above, based on the theory of communicative language ability, HSK 2.0 was designed to evaluate learners' language knowledge, as well as their ability to use language in communication. Besides, learners' ability of spoken expression and written expression has become the focus of HSK.

When designing HSK, various factors should be considered, including not only the test itself, but also the domestic and international demands, and actual situations. There is still a long way to expand the influence of HSK worldwide and establish HSK as an international brand. Many researchers pay attention to the promotion and development of HSK. For example, Luo et al. (2011a) analyzed the quality of HSK 2.0, with a focus on the degree of difficulty, distinction and reliability. He concluded that the overall difficulty of HSK was easier, which met the needs of Chinese language promotion and could encourage Chinese learners to continuously improve their Chinese language proficiency. The difficulty of each level of the test was set reasonably, and had a good degree of differentiation basically. Besides, Luo et al. (2011b) collected relevant data on the overseas promotion of HSK and made statistical analysis of candidates' gender, age and nationality, so as to provide a beneficial reference for the further promotion of HSK. Then, Zhao (2016) reviewed the related research on HSK and made a detailed and comprehensive presentation of the development of HSK in recent 30 years, which laid a solid foundation for the development of Chinese language.

The release of the *Standards* in 2021 has set out a discussion on the reform of HSK 2.0, and researchers believe that HSK 3.0 will be issued soon. Chinese Testing International (CTI) invited experts in the field of international Chinese language education, language assessment and linguistics, to discuss the research and development of HSK 3.0. The CTI (2021) made a summary of experts' opinions, which was presented as follows.

Based on HSK 2.0, HSK 3.0 should persist in evaluating test takers' communicative language ability. It should also demonstrate some innovative points, such as emphasizing the assessment of learners' integrated language skills and intercultural communicative competence. Besides, at the very beginning of developing HSK 3.0, researchers should describe the structure of the descriptors in the *Standards*, as well as compare the content of the *Standards* with that of the HSK 2.0 syllabus and test paper. And it's urgent to develop HSK Levels 7 to 9. (pp. 432)

To sum up, the content alignment made in the present study is necessary, and it will be beneficial for the refinement of HSK. In addition, since HSK only consists of six levels now, HSK Level 5 is relatively difficult. In this sense, the development of HSK Levels 7 to 9 will be inspired by the research on HSK Level 5.

7.3.2 The Construct of HSK

The development and reform of HSK indicate the construct of HSK. In other words, the construct of a test can be reflected by the process of test design.

Bachman(1990) proposed three basic steps for designing a test. The first step in designing a test was to distinguish the construct we wanted to measure from other similar constructs or to define the construct theoretically. He also pointed out that the content of language tests was based on either a theory of language proficiency or a specific domain of content, which was generally reflected by a course syllabus. According to Bachman, the second step in designing a test was defining the construct operationally, which required to relate the construct which is defined theoretically to the observations of behavior. In other words, making the construct observable is the purpose of this step. The third step in designing a test proposed by Bachman was quantifying the observations of performance according to scales. Bachman pointed out that those scales also reflected the construct of a test.

Besides, Zou (1998) mentioned that the test syllabus was considered as a reference for the test design, proposition, and evaluation. She also put forward that the test syllabus and item-writing manual affected the development of tests and had an influence on the rating criteria which represented the most specific descriptions of the construct that we wanted to measure.

Studies of both Bachman and Zou mentioned above indicate that materials related to the development of HSK, such as the curriculum syllabus, sample test papers, teaching syllabus and test syllabus, can reflect the guidelines and the construct of HSK. HSK should share a great number of similarities with the *Standards* from the content perspective, which can indicate a satisfactory degree of content alignment and is an important foundation of aligning studies. Content alignment is also regarded as a process of collecting evidence for construct validity. Therefore, making a comparison between those materials and language standards is a widely accepted method of content alignment.

7.3.3 HSK Level 5

HSK 2.0 was released in 2009, and it's still used today. HSK 2.0 consists of six levels. Compared with other levels of HSK, HSK Level 5 has the largest number of test takers (Fu et al., 2013).

In the field of language testing, the construct of a test refers to what a test is designed to measure (Bachman, 1990). The construct of HSK Level 5 is to evaluate learners' ability to use Chinese language from three dimensions: listening comprehension, reading comprehension and written expression, which explains the reason why HSK Level 5 includes listening, reading and writing subtests (Hanban, 2015; Fu et al., 2013).

According to *HSK Test Syllabus*, there are 100 tasks or items in HSK Level 5. Table 7.2 provides an overview of the content of HSK Level 5. Since the present study highlights the writing subtests of HSK Level 5, tasks in writing subtests will be introduced further. Section One of the writing subtest contains 8 tasks, and each task provides a few words from a sentence in a disordered order. Examinees are requested to put the given words in order logically and then complete sentences. In

Section Two, there are two tasks, Items 99 and 100 of HSK Level 5. Those two tasks require test takers to write a short passage according to several words or a picture provided.

Table 7.2 An Overview of the Content of HSK Level 5 (Hanban, 2015)

Tests content		The number of tasks or items
Listening subtests	Section One	20
	Section Two	25
Reading subtests	Section One	15
	Section Two	10
	Section Three	20
Writing subtests	Section One	8
	Section Two	2

Validity is an important factor concerning the quality of tests, and construct validity is the central concern of language testing research (Bachman, 1990). Fu et al. (2013) discussed the validity of HSK Level 5, with a focus on the internal structure of HSK Level 5. Results showed that the construct of HSK Level 5 was clear, and the validity of HSK Level 5 was relatively satisfactory. What is noteworthy is the findings about the first section of the writing subtest. To complete writing tasks in Section One, test takers should first understand the meaning of the words. The second thing was to be able to use these words to form sentences, which was based on the understanding of the meaning of sentences. Thirdly, they should have the ability to express themselves in a standardized way. The standardized way meant expressing in a correct word order. Fourthly, examinees were required to have the ability to transcribe Chinese characters. It showed that tasks in Section One were used to evaluate test takers' abilities of both reading comprehension and written expression. Because of the relatively poor quality of the writing tasks in Section One, they suggested that eight tasks in this section might be deleted in the future. Thus, the present study doesn't involve writing tasks in Section One.

Listening and reading are receptive language skills. There is a great deal of research on the quality of listening and reading subtests. When it comes to the listening subtest, Chen (2018) tried to explore its authenticity in light of the test materials and tasks and found that HSK Level 5 listening test was of high authenticity, but there still existed room for improvement. As for the reading subtest, Liu (2014) investigated its validity, and concluded that the reading subtest was of high validity.

Writing is a productive language skill. A number of researchers have showed their interest in HSK Level 5 writing test and pointed out the significance of writing tasks in HSK Level 5 in evaluating learners' writing ability. For example, Lu et al. (2012) proposed that different from the writing tasks in HSK Level 4, tasks in Level 5 required test takers to write a short passage, which evaluated learners' ability to write coherently and logically. And examinees should write a short passage according to several words or a picture given by writing tasks. Therefore, writing tasks in Level 5 also assessed learners' ability to understand the given materials, decide on proper topics, and write passages related to the decided topics. Based on the features of HSK writing tasks, Lu et al. gave suggestions on training students' Chinese writing, particularly on cultivating students' ability to use words and grammar properly and write cohesive and coherent paragraphs.

However, researchers have also pointed out shortcomings of HSK Level 5 writing test. For example, Bai et al. (2017) analyzed HSK Level 5 writing test and mentioned that its requirements on test takers' imagination and organizational competence made it difficult for test takers to complete.

In conclusion, the quality of HSK Level 5 is guaranteed, which is represented by the relatively good validity of HSK Level 5. HSK Level 5 writing test has attracted much attention during the past decades, and it contains two sections. The validity of the test concerned is an important foundation of aligning studies. Since the validity of tasks in Section One of HSK Level 5 writing test is unsatisfactory, the present study only focuses on the writing tasks in Section Two. Specifically, Items 99 and 100 are the focus of this study.

7.4 Research Questions

Compared with listening and reading subtests in the form of multiple-choice items, HSK writing subtests are relatively suitable for the evaluation of candidates' communicative language ability. HSK Level 5 test is the one with the largest number of candidates. Although the quality of HSK Level 5 is guaranteed, the construct of tasks in Section One of HSK Level 5 writing test is not our focus. Therefore, the present study only focuses on tasks in Section Two of HSK Level 5 writing test. The *Standards* formulated in the year 2021 are designed to evaluate the Chinese language proficiency of non-native speakers of Chinese, and they emphasize the characteristics of Chinese language. To sum up, the present study tries to align Items 99 and 100 of HSK Level 5 writing test with the *Standards*.

In terms of the aligning steps, similar to most aligning studies, the present study is designed on the basis of the *Manual* published by the Council of Europe. The content alignment or specification is the premise of standard setting. Hence, before allocating learners to different proficiency levels, the present study makes a content analysis in relation to the *Standards*, which is also considered as a process of collecting evidence for construct validity. But different from most aligning studies, the present study uses both qualitative and quantitative methods to make content alignment. Materials related to the construct of HSK, such as *HSK Rating Criteria*, *HSK Test Syllabus*, *HSK Test Item-Writing Manual*, as well as HSK sample tasks will be aligned with the *Standards*.

In the step of standard setting, the results of the content alignment will be corroborated, and performance standards will be set as well. Similar to most research on aligning tests of productive language skills with language standards, the present study adopts an examinee-centered method. However, the difference is that the judgment is made not only by experts, but also by

HSK Level 5 examinees, which improves the validity of this study. Specifically, examinees who have taken HSK Level 5 writing test need to evaluate the extent to which they can reach the requirements of the *Standards* Level 5. At the same time, experts are invited to align examinees' written scripts with the *Standards* Level 5. Based on their judgment, performance standards will be set. The validity of research materials and instruments is also the premise for the validity of this study. Besides, exploring the relation between examinees' self-evaluation data and their actual HSK scores, as well as the relation between experts' judgment and examinees' actual HSK scores, is the third way of collecting evidence for validity. In other words, the reliability of examinees' judgment and experts' judgment is analyzed in this way.

In conclusion, the present study aims at answering four research questions. On the one hand, from the content perspective, this study tries to explore: (1) What is the relation between *HSK Rating Criteria*, *HSK Test Syllabus* and *HSK Test Item-Writing Manual* for Items 99 and 100 of HSK Level 5, and the *Standards*? (2) To what extent can Items 99 and 100 of HSK Level 5 cover the requirements of the *Standards*? On the other hand, from the perspective of examinees' actual performance, this study tries to answer: (3) What is the relation between examinees' self-evaluation of their writing abilities based on the *Standards*, and their actual scores of Items 99 and 100 of HSK Level 5? (4) To what extent can Items 99 and 100 of HSK Level 5 be related to the *Standards*?

7.5 Summary

This chapter reviews studies of aligning, of the *Standards*, as well as of HSK. We can find that: (1) There is a lack of aligning Chinese language tests with Chinese-centered Chinese language standards. (2) Although most aligning studies take the *Manual* as a reference, methods of making content alignment and setting performance standards used in previous studies have still been highlighted and analyzed, due to the complexity and flexibility of aligning tests with language standards. Those methods are enlightening for the present study. (3) Both the *Standards* and HSK take the theory of communicative language ability as the theoretical grounding, which suggests a possibility of aligning HSK with the *Standards*. (4) The construct of HSK is reflected by *HSK Rating Criteria*, *HSK Test Syllabus*, *HSK Test Item-Writing Manual*, and HSK sample tasks. The conceptual framework of the *Standards* indicates the dimensions of making the content analysis of HSK. To sum up, the content of *HSK Rating Criteria*, *HSK Test Syllabus*, *HSK Test Item-Writing Manual*, and HSK sample tasks should be analyzed on the basis of the conceptual framework of the *Standards*, which serves as an important method of the content alignment.

8 Methodology

In this chapter, the following information will be introduced in detail. The working theoretical framework of the present study will be covered in the first section of this chapter. The second section is about the research design, including participants, instruments and materials, as well as aligning procedures and methods. The third section is about the data collection. The types of collected data and the process of collecting data will be explained. At the end of this chapter, methods of data analysis will be presented.

8.1 Working Theoretical Framework

The present study tries to align HSK Level 5 writing test with the *Standards* from the content and examinees' actual performance perspectives. Thus, as illustrated in Figure 8.1, the working theoretical framework of this study can be divided into two parts. One is about the content alignment, while the other is related to the performance standards.

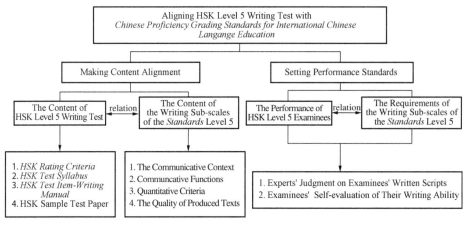

Figure 8.1 The Working Theoretical Framework of Present Study

When making a content alignment, the content of the test concerned will be analyzed in relation to the language standard in question. As mentioned in Chapter Two, the content of a test is reflected by its rating criteria, test syllabus, item-writing manual, as well as sample test papers, and the framework of the content analysis is designed on the basis of the structures of the language standard. Therefore, the content of HSK, including *HSK Rating Criteria*, *HSK Test Syllabus*, *HSK Test Item-Writing Manual*, as well as 3 sets of HSK sample test papers, is analyzed according to the content of the *Standards* in the present study.

As presented in Chapter Two, the content of the *Standards* can be analyzed from three aspects: (1) the communicative context described as different topics in descriptors, (2) the communicative functions described as communicative tasks in descriptors, and (3) the four-dimensional quantitative criteria representing the importance of Chinese language knowledge in communication. However, considering the objectives of the present study, characteristics of the writing sub-scales of the *Standards* should be considered as well. It is the quality of learners' performance on writing Chinese characters and writing compositions that the descriptors aim to describe (Center for Language Education and Cooperation, 2021b). Writing is a productive skill. The quality of learners' writing performance or the produced texts indicates their writing ability. In other words, levels of learners' writing ability are judged by the quality of the text they produce.

In conclusion, to make content alignment, the content of HSK should be analyzed from the following aspects: (1) the communicative context described as different topics in descriptors, (2) the communicative functions described as communicative tasks in descriptors, which indicates that writing can be regarded as an act of reaching a specific communicative purpose, (3) the four-dimensional quantitative criteria representing the importance of language knowledge in writing, and (4) the quality of produced texts indicating the quality of fulfillment of communicative tasks.

After making the content alignment, performance standards or cut-off scores will be set to differentiate examinees into different proficiency levels. When aligning tests of productive language skills with language standards, an examinee-centered method is usually adopted. Specifically, the examinee-centered method enables judges or participants to relate examinees' performance to the requirements of language standards. The performance of examinees is commonly considered as their written or oral production. Therefore, HSK Level 5 test takers' written scripts of Items 99 and 100 will be aligned with the requirements of the *Standards* in the present study.

The performance standards or cut-off scores are the test scores of the borderline examinee or the average scores of a group of borderline examinees. Borderline examinees refer to those who just meet the required proficiency level. Thus, a borderline examinee or a group of borderline examinees will be selected based on the judgment made by judges or participants. In this sense, an HSK Level 5 test taker or a group of HSK Level 5 test takers should be selected in the present study. According to judges' or participants' evaluation, the selected test taker or test takers just meet the requirements of the *Standards* Level 5.

Since the judges or participants of most aligning studies are experts, experts will be invited to judge the relation between HSK Level 5 test takers' written scripts and the *Standards* Level 5. However, the previous studies also suggest a student-centered method. Specifically, in addition to experts' judgment, performance standards or cut-off scores will also be set on the basis of examinees' self-evaluation of their language ability. Hence, the present study makes an adaption on the examinee-centered method, and HSK Level 5 test takers will be invited as judges or participants as well.

8.2 Research Design

To answer the four research questions, both qualitative and quantitative methods were employed in this study.

8.2.1 Participants

In this section, the coders who compared HSK Level 5 with the *Standards* from the content perspective, the experts who judged the content of HSK Level 5 and actual examinees' performance on HSK Level 5 writing test in a quantitative method, the interviewees who were invited to make comments on the relation between HSK Level 5 writing test and the *Standards*, as well as HSK Level 5 examinees who made a self-evaluation on their writing ability based on the *Standards* will be introduced.

8.2.1.1 Coders

Totally, there were two coders. One was the researcher herself, and the other was a postgraduate student pursuing the English and Chinese language testing as her research orientation. Both of the two coders made a qualitative content comparison between HSK Level 5 writing test and the *Standards* from four aspects: communicative functions, the communicative context, quantitative criteria and the quality of produced texts.

8.2.1.2 Experts

Overall, 55 wexe were invited to judge whether the HSK Level 5 writing test could be aligned or related to the *Standards* in terms of the content and actual examinees' performance.

Experts were selected in terms of their majors and research directions, so as to ensure that experts could use their professional knowledge when making the judgment. Among 55 experts, 8 majored in foreign linguistics and applied linguistics, and their research direction was about language testing and language education. The rest 47 majored in international Chinese language education.

Totally, experts were invited to analyze 3 sets of HSK Level 5 sample test papers (only including Items 99 and 100 of the writing section) in relation to the *Standards*. Besides, 30 examinees' scripts of Item 99 and 30 examinees' scripts of Item 100 were evaluated in relation to the *Standards* as well.

In terms of the content comparison, each of the 55 experts was invited to assess all the HSK Level 5 sample test papers. However, only 30 of the 55 experts judged the relation between examinees' scripts and the *Standards*.

Those 30 experts were equally divided into two groups, i.e. Group 1 and Group 2. Each member of Group 1 evaluated 6 scripts of Item 99, while each expert of Group 2 judged 6 scripts of Item 100. To ensure validity, each script should be evaluated by 3 experts. And before they made the final judgment, they should not discuss it with each other. Therefore, experts in Group 1 and Group 2 were further divided into 5 teams. In each team, there were 3 experts, and they judged the same 6 scripts. Table 8.1 presents a description of those 30 experts who judge the relation between scripts and the *Standards*.

Table 8.1 A Description of Experts Judging Scripts in Relation to the *Standards*

Groups	Teams	Members	Scripts to be judged
1	1	3 experts	6 scripts of Item 99
	2	3 experts	6 scripts of Item 99
	3	3 experts	6 scripts of Item 99
	4	3 experts	6 scripts of Item 99
	5	3 experts	6 scripts of Item 99
2	1	3 experts	6 scripts of Item 100
	2	3 experts	6 scripts of Item 100
	3	3 experts	6 scripts of Item 100
	4	3 experts	6 scripts of Item 100
	5	3 experts	6 scripts of Item 100

8.2.1.3 Interviewees

In total, 4 experts (Interviewee A, Interviewee B, Interviewee C and Interviewee D) voluntarily took part in interviews. Two of them (Interviewee A and Interviewee B) made comments on Item 99 of HSK Level 5, while the other two experts (Interviewee C and Interviewee D) were asked about Item 100 of HSK Level 5. Those four experts were selected based on their judgment on Item 99 or 100 in terms of the content and actual examinees' performance. In addition, they had research experience related to International Chinese language education and had professional background of language testing.

To ensure the quality of interviews, the researcher designed an interview outline according to the judgment made by those 4 experts. The outline was sent to experts online in advance. Besides, 4 experts were interviewed one by one in order to lower the influence of irrelevant factors. Due to the time and space limitation, interviews were held online.

8.2.1.4 Examinees

276 examinees who had taken and passed HSK Level 5 writing test answered an online self-evaluation questionnaire. They were invited to judge their own Chinese writing ability based on the descriptors in the *Standards*.

The selection of examinees, as well as the release of the self-evaluation questionnaire were supported by the Center for Language Education and Cooperation, which is affiliated with the Ministry of Education of the People's Republic of China. As presented on its official website, the Center for Language Education and Cooperation is committed to providing quality services for people worldwide to learn Chinese language and understand China, as well as to building a friendly and collaborative platform for the exchange and cooperation between China and foreign countries and for the mutual appreciation of diverse cultures around the world. Thus, the quality of those selected examinees and the release of the questionnaire were ensured. In addition, a written description or instruction was provided to make sure that examinees could understand what they needed to do.

The self-evaluation questionnaire for HSK Level 5 test takers was bilingual, and designed in 8 versions, specifically including Chinese-English, Chinese-Thai, Chinese-French, Chinese-Japanese, Chinese-Korean, Chinese-Arabic, Chinese-Spanish and Chinese-Russian versions. A description of the 276 examinees who answered the questionnaire is presented in Table 8.2.

Table 8.2 A Description of the Examinees

Chinese-English/%	Chinese-Thai/%	Chinese-Spanish/%	Chinese-Japanese/%	Chinese-Russian/%	Chinese-French/%	Chinese-Arabic/%	Chinese-Korean/%
52 (18.84)	17 (6.16)	4 (1.45)	30 (10.87)	3 (1.09)	4 (1.45)	40 (14.49)	126 (45.65)

Although 276 examinees answered the questionnaire, the questionnaire data of only 196 examinees was used to answer the research question. The third research question aims at exploring the relation between examinees' self-evaluation of their writing ability based on the *Standards*, and their actual scores of Items 99 and 100 of HSK Level 5. The final results of this question also serve as the reliability indices of examinees' self-evaluation, and based on reliable self-evaluation data, cut-off scores will be provided as performance standards to differentiate examinees. Thus, those 276 examinees' HSK scores were then searched by their candidate numbers entered in the questionnaire. However, 80 of them did not provide correct candidate numbers, which brought difficulty in searching their actual HSK test scores. In other words, scores of only 196 examinees could be found.

8.2.2 Instruments and Materials

This section mainly presents the instruments and materials of this study, including the self-evaluation questionnaires for examinees, the questionnaires for experts, the interview outline and recording equipment, as well as the materials to be judged.

8.2.2.1 The Self-evaluation Questionnaires for Examinees

Since December 2019, the present researcher has been working in an empirical study on the validity of the *Standards*. A large-scale questionnaire survey is one of the main research methods. Members of the project team made joint efforts to design questionnaires from December 2019 to April 2020.

The *Standards* divided learners' Chinese language ability into 3 levels and 9 bands. As a result, 9 questionnaires corresponding to the 9 bands of the

Standards were designed totally. Furthermore, due to the structure of descriptors in each band, the construct of those 9 questionnaires was the Chinese language abilities described by the *Standards*, including 5 language skills (listening comprehension, spoken expression, reading comprehension, written expression, translation and interpretation), verbal communication abilities, and quantitative criteria.

The number of items in questionnaires of bands 1, 2 and 3 was 49. The number of items in questionnaires of bands 4, 5, 6, 7, 8 and 9 was 59. Table 8.3 provides an overview of the structure of those 9 questionnaires. All items in those 9 questionnaires were based on the descriptors in the *Standards*. Most of them were in the form of Likert 5-point scales, except items 22, 23, 48 and 49 in questionnaires of bands 1, 2 and 3, as well as items 58 and 59 in questionnaires of bands 4, 5, 6, 7, 8 and 9. Choices 0 to 4 of Likert 5-point scale questions referred to "totally untrue" "hardly true" "basically true" "largely true" and "totally true".

Table 8.3 An Overview of the Structure of Self-evaluation Questionnaires

Band	LC	SE	RC	WE	TI	VCA	QC
1	1-10	11-20	21-30	31-40	0	41-45	46-49
2	1-10	11-20	21-30	31-40	0	41-45	46-49
3	1-10	11-20	21-30	31-40	0	41-45	46-49
4	1-10	11-20	21-30	31-40	41-50	51-55	56-59
5	1-10	11-20	21-30	31-40	41-50	51-55	56-59
6	1-10	11-20	21-30	31-40	41-50	51-55	56-59
7	1-10	11-20	21-30	31-40	41-50	51-55	56-59
8	1-10	11-20	21-30	31-40	41-50	51-55	56-59
9	1-10	11-20	21-30	31-40	41-50	51-55	56-59

Note: LC: listening comprehension; SE: spoken expression; RC: reading comprehension; WE: written expression; TI: translation and interpretation; VCA: verbal communication abilities; QC: quantitative criteria

To improve the validity of those questionnaires, it is necessary to ensure a relatively reasonable structure of those questionnaires. Requirements of items should also be stated in a clear way to make sure that participants can understand what they need to do and then give an appropriate response. In this case, before the distribution of those questionnaires, experts were invited to go through them, and a trial test was also conducted. According to the data from the trial test, the questionnaires were revised several times. The final drafts of those questionnaires were finished in March 2020.

Then, from March to April in 2020, those questionnaires were translated into 8 languages, including English, French, Spanish, Japanese, Korean, Russian, Thai and Arabic. The translators were mainly local experts in international Chinese language education in the respective countries, taking the above languages as their native languages.

Supported by the Center for Language Education and Cooperation, the questionnaires were distributed to authorized HSK test centers and schools in the mainland of China and 23 countries in 6 regions, including Asia, Europe and Oceania. A total of 2086 International Chinese language learners from 38 countries around the world answered the bilingual questionnaires (Chinese and foreign languages) in 8 bilingual versions, including the Chinese-English, Chinese-Thai, Chinese-French, Chinese-Japanese, Chinese-Korean, Chinese-Arabic, Chinese-Spanish, as well as Chinese-Russian versions. Finally, we obtained 2520 valid questionnaire data from 37 countries for the 9 bands.

The present study only focused on the questionnaire of Band 5. 276 examinees who had sat for HSK Level 5 were invited to answer this questionnaire, and evaluated their Chinese language ability based on the *Standards*. As an example, the Chinese-English version of this questionnaire is presented in Appendix A. Items 1 to 10 aim at evaluating examinees' Chinese language ability of written expression. Considering the objectives of the present study, examinees' answers to those 10 items will be analyzed in this aligning study.

The validity of research instruments has a great influence on this aligning study. The validity of the questionnaire of Band 5 is verified by a factor analysis since all items of the questionnaire are based on the descriptors in the *Standards*. Seven factors are expected to be extracted. They are listening comprehension, spoken expression, reading comprehension, written expression, translation and interpretation, verbal communication ability and quantitative criteria.

Table 8.4　KMO and Bartlett's Test of the Self-evaluation Questionnaire ($n=276$)

Kaiser-Meyer-Olkin Measure of Sampling Adequacy	Bartlett's Test of Sphericity		
	Approx. Chi-Square	df	Sig.
0.977	21,742.193	1,711	0.000

The results illustrated in Table 8.4 ensure the feasibility of a factor analysis. The value of KMO is 0.977 which is obviously higher than 0.9. In addition, the value of sig. is lower than 0.05. It means that a correlation exists among all items.

According to Table 8.5, the total initial eigenvalue of 5 components or factors are higher than 1. Besides, the cumulative variance contribution rate of all those 7 factors is 77.415%. The results shown in Table 8.5 verify the satisfactory validity of this self-evaluation questionnaire.

The reliability of the self-evaluation questionnaire is reflected by the correlation between examinees' self-evaluation data and their actual HSK scores, which is exactly what the third research question focuses on. As mentioned before, the final results of the third research question serve as the reliability indices of examinees' self-evaluation, and based on the reliable self-evaluation data, cut-off scores will be provided as performance standards to differentiate examinees. Thus, instead of being presented in this section, the reliability of the self-evaluation questionnaire is reported in the next Chapter in detail.

Table 8.5 Total Variance Explained of the Self-evaluation Questionnaire ($n=276$)

Components	Initial Eigenvalues			Extraction Sums of Squared Loadings			Rotation Sums of Squared Loadings		
	Total	% of Variance	Cumulative %	Total	% of Variance	Cumulative %	Total	% of Variance	Cumulative %
1	39.676	67.248	67.248	39.676	67.248	67.248	12.101	20.510	20.510
2	1.942	3.292	70.540	1.942	3.292	70.540	11.373	19.276	39.785
3	1.731	2.935	73.474	1.731	2.935	73.474	10.868	18.420	58.206
4	1.305	2.213	75.687	1.305	2.213	75.687	8.554	14.498	72.704
5	1.1019	1.728	77.415	1.019	1.728	77.415	2.779	4.710	77.415
6	0.832	1.410	78.825						
7	0.815	1.381	80.205						
8	0.645	1.109	81.314						

8.2.2.2 The Questionnaires for Experts

Totally, 11 questionnaires for experts were designed by the present research team. Similar to the self-questionnaires for examinees, all items of the questionnaires for experts were also based on the descriptors in the *Standards*. 36 items existed in each of those 11 questionnaires. All items were in the form of Likert 5-point scales. Choices 1 to 5 referred to "totally untrue" "hardly true" "basically true" "largely true" and "totally true". Table 8.6 gives a description of those 11 questionnaires.

Questionnaire 1 (see Appendix B) required experts to judge 6 sample tasks (Tasks 1 – 6) chosen from 3 sets of HSK Level 5 sample test papers in relation to 6 descriptors (Descriptors 1 – 6) in the writing sub-scales of the *Standards* Level 5. Questionnaires 2 to 6 focused on the relation between 30 examinees' scripts of Item 99 (Scripts 1 – 30) and the 6 descriptors (Descriptors 1 – 6), while Questionnaires 7 to 11 highlighted the relation between 30 examinees' scripts of Item 100 (Scripts 31 – 60) and the 6 descriptors (Descriptors 1 – 6). Take Questionnaire 2 and Questionnaire 7 as examples (see Appendix C). And Table 8.7 provides an overview of the structure of those 3 questionnaires (Questionnaires 1, 2 and 7).

Totally, 55 experts answered Questionnaire 1. In terms of the 11 questionnaires used to collect experts' judgment on examinees' written scripts in relation to the *Standards*, each of them was answered by 3 experts.

Before the distribution of those questionnaires, a pilot test was conducted. According to the data from the pilot test, questionnaires had been revised several times before the final drafts of those questionnaires were finished in October 2021.

The reliability of the questionnaires for experts was analyzed by the correlation between experts' judgment and the actual scores of scripts. When answering Research Question Four, performance standards or cut-off scores should be set on the basis of reliable experts' judgment. Hence, instead of being presented in this section, the reliability of the questionnaires for experts is reported in the next chapter in detail.

Table 8.6 A Description of the Questionnaires for Experts

Questionnaire	Focus	Participants	The number of items
1	Tasks 1 - 6	55 experts	36
2	Scripts 1 - 6	3 experts of Team 1, Group 1	36
3	Scripts 7 - 12	3 experts of Team 2, Group 1	36
4	Scripts 13 - 18	3 experts of Team 3, Group 1	36
5	Scripts 19 - 24	3 experts of Team 4, Group 1	36
6	Scripts 25 - 30	3 experts of Team 5, Group 1	36
7	Scripts 31 - 36	3 experts of Team 1, Group 2	36
8	Scripts 37 - 42	3 experts of Team 2, Group 2	36
9	Scripts 43 - 48	3 experts of Team 3, Group 2	36
10	Scripts 49 - 54	3 experts of Team 4, Group 2	36
11	Scripts 55 - 60	3 experts of Team 5, Group 2	36

Table 8.7 An Overview of the Structure of the Questionnaires for Experts

Questionnaire	Items 1 - 6	Items 7 - 12	Items 13 - 18	Items 19 - 24	Items 25 - 30	Items 31 - 36
1	Task 1	Task 2	Task 3	Task 4	Task 5	Task 6
2	Script 1	Script 2	Script 3	Script 4	Script 5	Script 6
7	Script 31	Script 32	Script 33	Script 34	Script 35	Script 36

8.2.2.3 The Interview Outline and Recording Equipment

After analyzing the judgment made by the four chosen experts, the researcher designed an interview outline (see Appendix D), and sent it to experts at least one day before the interview. Thus, experts had enough time to prepare.

Tencent Meeting is an application ensuring the possibility of having interviews online and making the record at the same time. Besides, the researcher can share her screen and present materials vividly and conveniently. Therefore, interviews were all held online by using Tencent Meeting.

Considering the potential differences between Item 99 and Item 100, and distinctions among experts, interviews were not conducted exactly as outlined. Some changes were made by the researcher during the interviews, to dig out the underlying reasons for experts' judgment.

8.2.2.4 The Materials to be Judged

Table 8.8 presents the materials to be judged by participants and their sources. There are eight materials, including the sample test paper, examinees' scripts and their scores, *HSK Rating Criteria*, *HSK Test Syllabus*, *HSK Test Item-Writing Manual* and the *Standards*.

As mentioned before, the present researchers have been working on a project supported by the Center for Language Education and Cooperation since December 2019. The project is about an empirical study on the validity of *Chinese Proficiency Grading Standards for International Chinese Language Education*. Thus, the researcher submitted a data request in March 2021. Then the first six materials in Table 8.8 were directly provided by the Center for Language Education and Cooperation.

Only Items 99 and 100 of the 3 sets of HSK Level 5 sample test papers were used in this study. Totally, 6 sample tasks needed to be judged. Table 8.9 provides an overview of those 6 writing tasks.

Table 8.8 Material to be Judged by Participants

Number	Materials	Sources
1	3 sets of HSK Level 5 sample test papers	The Center for Language Education and Cooperation
2	196 examinees' scores of HSK Level 5 writing test	
3	30 examinees' scripts of Item 99 and their scores	
4	30 examinees' scripts of Item 100 and their scores	
5	*HSK Rating Criteria*	
6	*HSK Test Item-Writing Manual*	
7	*HSK Test Syllabus*	Downloaded online (http://www.chinesetest.cn)
8	the *Standards*	Downloaded online (http://www.moe.gov.cn/)

Table 8.9 A Description of the Six Writing Tasks

Task	Writing tasks
Task 1	The Item 99 in the first set of test paper
Task 2	The Item 100 in the first set of test paper
Task 3	The Item 99 in the second set of test paper
Task 4	The Item 100 in the second set of test paper
Task 5	The Item 99 in the third set of test paper
Task 6	The Item 100 in the third set of test paper

As mentioned before, examinees' scores of Items 99 and 100 were searched by their candidate numbers entered in the self-evaluation questionnaire. 276 examinees answered the self-evaluation questionnaire. However, 80 of them did not provide correct candidate numbers, which brought difficulty in searching their actual HSK test scores. Therefore, the Center for Language Education and Cooperation could only provide HSK Level 5 scores of 196 examinees. The writing scripts of those 196 examinees were double-rated, which could improve the validity and reliability.

The examinees' scripts of Items 99 and 100 were also judged. Totally, 30 scripts(Scripts 1 – 30) of Item 99, along with 30 scripts (Scripts 31 – 60) of Item 100 were chosen by the Center for Language Education and Cooperation. The scores of those 60 scripts were provided as well. Besides, *HSK Rating Criteria*, and *HSK Test Item-Writing Manual* were also given by the Center for Language Education and Cooperation.

HSK Test Syllabus, and the *Standards* were downloaded on the official websites by the researcher herself. Considering the objectives of this study, only the 6 descriptors involved in the writing sub-scales of the *Standards* Level 5 were used. Table 8.10 provides a description of those 6 descriptors.

Table 8.10 Descriptors in the Writing Sub-scales of the *Standards* Level 5

Number	Descriptors
1	Can master the 250 Chinese characters in the List of Handwritten Chinese Characters of the Intermediate Level.
2	Can use comparatively complex sentence patterns to write paragraphs.
3	Can analyze the structure of common Chinese characters.
4	Can complete common narratives, expositions and argumentations, etc. of no less than 450 Chinese characters in a limited time.
5	Can complete writing tasks with comparatively appropriate vocabulary, basically correct sentence patterns, comparatively complete content, and comparatively clear expression.
6	Can complete common practical forms of writing in Chinese with basically correct format and basically standard expression.

8.2.3 Research Procedures and Methods

In the present study, aligning refers to aligning HSK Level 5 writing test with the *Standards* by analyzing the content of HSK Level 5 writing test in relation to the *Standards*, and setting performance standards. Referring to the aligning steps in the *Manual*, the present study made an adaption. Figure 8.2 presents the aligning procedure and methods of the present study.

The first step of aligning was the familiarization. Having all the activities mentioned in the *Manual* will take several hours. Those activities require preparation, and keeping them relatively simple remains a problem as well. Hence, the researcher did not adopt those activities.

Considering the objectives of this study, the researcher decided to present descriptors involved in the writing sub-scales of the *Standards*, and experts were invited to read those descriptors in order to refresh their knowledge and ensure their familiarity with the *Standards*. Besides, the researchers introduced and explained the procedure and requirements of this aligning study. Activities designed in the step of familiarization improved the validity of this study.

The second step was the specification or content alignment. The content of HSK Level 5 writing test was analyzed in relation to the *Standards*.

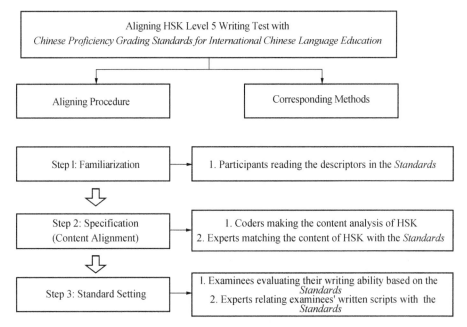

Figure 8.2　Aligning Procedures and Methods of the Present Study

Different from most aligning studies, the present study adopted both qualitative and quantitative methods.

As for the quantitative method, the questionnaire survey was adopted. A questionnaire was designed to collect experts' judgment on the extent to which the content of 3 sets of HSK Level 5 sample test papers could be aligned with the *Standards*.

In terms of the qualitative method, the content of *HSK Rating Criteria*, *HSK Test Syllabus* and *HSK Test Item-Writing Manual* was analyzed by the researcher herself and a postgraduate student from four dimensions: quantitative criteria, communicative functions, the communicative context and the quality of produced texts. After that, an interview survey was adopted to have a further analysis of experts' judgment collected by the questionnaire.

The third step was the standard setting. Performance standards were set in this step. Different from most aligning studies, both examinees themselves and experts were participants. Besides, the present study adopted both quantitative and qualitative methods.

Specifically, HSK Level 5 examinees evaluated their writing ability based on the *Standards* by answering the self-evaluation questionnaire. Meanwhile, experts judged the degree of linkage between examinees' written scripts of Items 99 and 100 and the *Standards* by answering questionnaires. Besides, an interview survey was then adopted to make a further analysis of experts' judgment collected by the questionnaires.

Based on examinees' self-evaluation and experts' judgment, cut-off scores were be provided as a reference for allocating HSK Level 5 examinees to different proficiency levels of the *Standards*, or served as a reference for deciding whether they could reach the requirements of descriptors in the writing sub-scales of the *Standards* Level 5.

The questionnaires used in the step of standard setting were all designed on the basis of the descriptors in the *Standards* Level 5. Because most methods introduced by the *Manual* do not contribute to discovering the specific and detailed alignment between tests and each descriptor in language standards, which usually leads to difficulty in ensuring the validity of the aligning research (Harsch et al., 2015). For example, some methods of setting performance standards, such as the Tucker-Angoff method, Yes-No method and extended Tucker-Angoff method, require participants to imagine a minimally acceptable person or borderline person, which leads to the difficulty for participants to have a shared understanding of this abstract person. In addition, some methods, such as the Tucker-Angoff method and extended Tucker-Angoff method, require participants to estimate the possibility of answering test items correctly, which will lead to unreliable results.

Evidence for the validity should be collected during the whole process of this aligning study. The selection and training of participants, the design of research instruments, and the quality of the materials to be judged affect the validity of this study. Those factors have already been controlled and explained before. Besides, to improve the validity of content alignment, both quantitative and qualitative methods were used to analyze multiple materials about HSK Level 5 writing test. The validity of standard setting was ensured by inviting both examinees and experts to make the judgment, as well as by exploring the correlations between their judgments and actual HSK scores.

8.3 Data Collection

There were two types of data: the quantitative and qualitative data, which were collected by the qualitative content analysis, questionnaires and interviews. The process of the data collection is then introduced.

8.3.1 Types of Data

Table 8.11 presents a summary of the types of data, and gives a detailed description. Both quantitative and qualitative data were collected. In terms of the qualitative data, they were collected by content analysis and interviews. As for quantitative data, they were collected by questionnaires.

Table 8.11 Types of Data Collected in the Present study

Data	Detailed description
Qualitative data	• The content analysis of *HSK Rating Criteria*, *HSK Test Syllabus*, and *HSK Test Item-Writing Manual* • Interviews about experts' judgment on HSK sample tasks, examinees' written scripts and the *Standards*
Quantitative data	• Examinees' self-evaluation of their writing ability • Experts' judgment on the content of Items 99 and 100 in relation to the *Standards* • Experts' judgment on HSK Level 5 examinees' written scripts of Items 99 and 100 in relation to the *Standards* • Examinees' actual scores of Items 99 and 100

8.3.2 The Process of Data Collection

As mentioned before, supported by the Center for Language Education and Cooperation, examinees' self-evaluation data was collected in the year 2020. The questionnaires for experts were full of Likert 5-point scale questions. Before distributing the questionnaires to experts, the researchers made a trail test, and collected suggestions on the questionnaires. Based on those suggestions, the researchers made adjustments. After that, the questionnaires were officially distributed.

The whole process of collecting experts' judgment can be broken into two stages. The first stage was conducted in November 2021. 33 first-year graduate students took part in the research. The researchers contacted the instructor of those students in advance, and obtained the permission to enter the classrooms and introduced the research. However, because of the insufficient amount of data, the second stage was then conducted in January 2022. This time, 22 second-year graduate students joined this study.

To improve the validity of this aligning study, before providing questionnaires to experts, the researchers introduced the process of this study, and explained the requirements on experts made by questionnaires. Besides, to refresh experts' knowledge and ensure their degree of familiarity with the *Standards*, the researchers presented the descriptors involved in the writing sub-scales of the *Standards*, and the experts were invited to read those descriptors before answering the questionnaires.

As for the qualitative data, results of the content analysis were produced in October 2021. Before making the content analysis, one of the researchers and another coder had a discussion, and reached the consensus on the analysis dimensions. Then, they made the content analysis without any discussion. After that, they discussed the differences between their coding until a consensus was reached. Finally, the researchers made a summary, and provided the final results. In order to make the results more reliable, the results were checked for a second time. The interviews were held online in January 2022.

8.4 Data Analysis

The study used both qualitative and quantitative analysis to answer the four research questions. Table 8.12 illustrates the methods of analyzing the data collected in the present study.

Table 8.12　Analysis Methods Utilized

Research Questions	Data	Methods
Q1: What is the relation between *HSK Rating Criteria*, *HSK Test Syllabus* and *HSK Test Item-Writing Manual* for Items 99 and 100 of HSK Level 5, and the *Standards*?	Qualitative data	Content analysis
Q2: To what extent can Items 99 and 100 of HSK Level 5 cover requirements of the *Standards*?	1. Likert 5-point scales data 2. Interview data	1. Descriptive statistics 2. One-way ANOVA 3. Post-hoc test
Q3: What is the relation between examinees' self-evaluation of their writing abilities based on the *Standards*, and their actual scores of Items 99 and 100 of HSK Level 5?	1. Likert 5-point scales data 2. Examinees' scores of Items 99 and 100	1. Descriptive statistics 2. Correlation analysis 3. Regression analysis
Q4: To what extent can Items 99 and 100 of HSK Level 5 be related with the *Standards*?	1. Likert 5-point scales data 2. Examinees' scores of Items 99 and 100 3. Interview data	1. Descriptive statistics 2. One-way ANOVA 3. Post-hoc test

9 Results

This chapter mainly presents the results for each of the research questions. The related statistical findings are given to answer the four research questions. Notably, if it is necessary, a descriptive statistical analysis is made before any inferential statistical analysis.

9.1 Results for Research Question One

A qualitative method was employed to answer the first research question. To be specific, the content of *HSK Rating Criteria*, *HSK Test Syllabus*, and *HSK Test Item-Writing Manual* was discussed in relation to the *Standards*. The framework of the content analysis were mentioned in Chapter 8. To be specific, the content of *HSK Rating Criteria*, *HSK Test Syllabus* and *HSK Test Item-Writing Manual* was analyzed from four dimensions: quantitative criteria, communicative functions, communicative context and quality of produced texts.

Results of this research question suggest the possibility and feasibility of aligning Items 99 and 100 of HSK Level 5 writing test with the *Standards* from the perspectives of the content and the actual examinees' performance.

Combining the judgment made by the researcher herself and another postgraduate student, the researcher made a summary. The final results are reported as follows.

9.1.1 Quantitative Criteria

The quantitative criteria mentioned in the writing sub-scales of the *Standards* represents the importance of language knowledge in writing, including learners' knowledge of syllables, Chinese characters, words and phrases, as well as the grammar.

Table 9.1 shows the detailed corresponding contents in the *Standards*, *HSK Rating Criteria*, *HSK Test Syllabus* and *HSK Test Item-Writing Manual*. Two descriptors in the writing sub-scales of the *Standards* highlight learners' knowledge of Chinese characters. Descriptions of quantitative criteria, especially of words and phrases, can be found in *HSK Test Syllabus* and *HSK Test Item-Writing Manual*.

Table 9.1 The Comparison from the Quantitative Criteria Aspect

Material	Corresponding Contents
The *Standards*	Can master 2,500 Chinese characters in the List of handwritten Chinese characters of the Intermediate Level (Center for Language Education and Cooperation, 2021b). Can analyze the structure of common Chinese characters (Center for Language Education and Cooperation, 2021b).
HSK Rating Criteria	No corresponding contents can be found.
HSK Test Syllabus	HSK Level 5 is designed for learners who have already mastered 2,500 common words and phrases.
HSK Test Item-Writing Manual	The number of words and phrases required by HSK (Level 5) is 2,500. Based on the 1,200 words and phrases required by HSK (Level 4), 1,300 new words and phrases are added. When designing test questions, test developers should limit the number of words beyond the requirement to about 15%. In principle, each question should contain as many new words and phrases (1,300) as possible to ensure the difficulty of the test questions and the test paper. In principle, words and phrases which are tested or used in question options should be within the range of requirements (2,500 words and phrases). Totally, 5 words and phrases are provided in Item 99. At least three of them should be selected from the 1,300 new words and phrases. Besides, those 5 words and phrases should also be selected with a variety of chapters of speech, including nouns, verbs and adjectives.

9.1.2 Communicative Functions

The communicative functions are described as communicative tasks in descriptors in the writing sub-scales of the *Standards*, which indicates that writing can be regarded as an act of reaching a specific communicative purpose.

Table 9.2 presents specific corresponding contents in the *Standards*, *HSK Rating Criteria*, *HSK Test Syllabus* and *HSK Test Item-writing Manual*. Three descriptors in the *Standards* describe learners' ability to write paragraphs, as well as write narrative, expository, argumentative, and practical passages. In *HSK Rating Criteria*, the completion of tasks is regarded as an important factor in the scoring scripts, and the communicative purposes of writing are also highlighted. According to statements in *HSK Test Syllabus*, examinees are required to write a short passage, which shows the communicative functions of writing. In *HSK Test Item-Writing Manual*, the test paper and test tasks are designed with a focus on evaluating learners' communicative ability, so the corpus of HSK should be beneficial for examinees to complete communicative tasks.

Table 9.2 The Comparison from the Communicative Functions Aspect

Material	Corresponding Contents
The *Standards*	Can use comparatively complex sentence patterns to write paragraphs (Center for Language Education and Cooperation, 2021b). Can complete common narratives, expositions and argumentations, etc. of no less than 450 Chinese characters in a limited time (Center for Language Education and Cooperation, 2021b). Can complete common practical forms of writing in Chinese.
HSK Rating Criteria	Examinees' scripts should be rated from the contents, structures, as well as the completion of tasks and communicative purposes. Examinees should complete the tasks required by test questions. All the words provided in test questions can be found in their scripts, or the contents of their scripts can be matched with the topics of the picture provided. There are several errors in the use of words and phrases, but they do not affect the completion of communication purposes.

continued

Material	Corresponding Contents
HSK Test Syllabus	The second chapter consists of 2 questions. The first question provides several words and phrases, and requires candidates to use those words and phrases to write a short passage of about 80 Chinese characters. The second question provides a picture, and candidates need to write a short passage of about 80 Chinese characters according to the picture.
HSK Test Item-Writing Manual	HSK is mainly aimed at evaluating learners' communicative ability, so the corpus of HSK tests should be selected in terms of its communicative functions. The picture provided in Item 100 should contribute to stimulating candidates' imagination, recall and description. Thus, candidates can write a passage based on the picture.

9.1.3 Communicative Context

The communicative context is described as different topics in descriptors in the writing sub-scales of the *Standards*, which suggests that communicative tasks are always fulfilled in a specific context.

Table 9.3 provides a summary of the statements of the communicative context in the *Standards*, *HSK Rating Criteria*, *HSK Test Syllabus* and *HSK Test Item-Writing Manual*. According to the three descriptors in the writing sub-scales of the *Standards*, learners are required to fulfill communicative tasks, such as writing a short passage, in a common context. According to the *HSK Rating Criteria*, topics of examinees' scripts are affected by topics of the pictures provided by test tasks, or by topics indicated by the provided words. The statements in the *HSK Test Syllabus* also indicate that topics of examinees' scripts are affected by the words and phrases, or the pictures provided by test tasks. Besides, considering the statements in the *HSK Test Item-Writing Manual*, the words provided in Item 99, and the picture provided in Item 100 should be selected around specific topics.

Table 9.3 The Comparison from the Communicative Context Aspect

Material	Corresponding Contents
The *Standards*	Can use comparatively complex sentence patterns to write paragraphs (Center for Language Education and Cooperation, 2021b). Can complete common narratives, expositions and argumentations, etc. in a limited time (Center for Language Education and Cooperation, 2021b). Can complete common practical forms of writing in Chinese (Center for Language Education and Cooperation, 2021b).
HSK Rating Criteria	All the words provided in test questions can be found in examinees' scripts, or the contents of their scripts can be matched with the topics of the picture provided. There are several errors in the use of words and phrases, but they do not affect the fulfillment of communicative tasks.
HSK Test Syllabus	The second chapter consists of 2 questions. The first question provides several words, and requires candidates to use those words and phrases to write a short passage of about 80 Chinese characters. The second question provides a picture, and asks candidates to write a short passage of about 80 Chinese characters based on the picture.
HSK Test Item-Writing Manual	HSK is mainly aimed at evaluating learners' communicative ability, so the corpus of HSK should be selected in terms of its communicative functions. The 5 words provided in Item 99 should be selected around a certain topic. The picture provided in Item 100 should contribute to stimulating candidates' imagination, recall and description. Thus, candidates can write a passage based on the picture.

9.1.4 Quality of Produced Texts

In terms of the quality of produced texts or the quality of the fulfillment of communicative tasks, the *Standards* is related to the other two materials. The content of *HSK Rating Criteria*, and *HSK Test Syllabus* can be matched with the *Standards* from the perspective of the quality of produced texts.

1) The *Standards*

Can complete common narratives, expositions, and argumentations, etc. of no less than 450 Chinese characters in a limited time (Center for Language Education and Cooperation, 2021a).

Can complete writing tasks with comparatively appropriate vocabulary, basically correct sentence patterns, comparatively complete content, and comparatively clear expression (Center for Language Education and Cooperation, 2021a).

Can complete common practical forms of writing in Chinese with basically correct format and basically standard expression (Center for Language Education and Cooperation, 2021a).

2) *HSK Rating Criteria*

At the beginning of scoring scripts, raters should allocate those scripts to five major grades (Grades 1 to 5) on the basis of the overall content and structure, as well as the completion of tasks and communicative purposes, and then, scores (0 to 21 points) are awarded on the basis of the accuracy and richness of words and phrases, as well as grammar points.

For example, a short passage allocated to Grade 5 should meet the following requirements:

(1) The overall content and structure: The short passage is relatively full and logical in its content, complete and clear in its structure and organization, as well as smooth and appropriate in its expression. Candidates can meet the requirements of test items, which means that all the words provided in Item 99 can be found in their scripts, or the content of their scripts can be matched with the topic of the picture provided in Item 100. The short passage contains no less than 60 Chinese characters.

(2) The grammar: It's fluent and expressive. Complex sentence structures can be found in it. It is also grammatically accurate, with no simple grammatical errors, especially in the use of function words and word order.

(3) The words and phrases: Various words and phrases are used in the script accurately and appropriately. Several errors which do not affect the completion of communicative tasks are allowed. One or two wrongly written Chinese characters are allowed.

3) *HSK Test Syllabus*

The second part consists of 2 items. The first item provides several words and phrases, and requires candidates to use those words and phrases to write a short passage of about 80 Chinese characters. The second item provides a picture, and asks candidates to write a short passage of about 80 Chinese characters according to the picture.

4) *HSK Test Item-Writing Manual*

No corresponding contents can be found.

9.1.5 Summary

Table 9.4 summarizes the results of the content analysis. If there exists a matching relationship, then a tick (√) will be placed in the corresponding box. The construct of HSK is reflected by *HSK Rating Criteria*, *HSK Test Syllabus*, and *HSK Test Item-Writing Manual*. HSK Level 5 writing test can be related to the *Standards* in terms of quantitative criteria, communicative functions, communicative context, and quality of produced texts. Thus, it is feasible and possible to align Items 99 and 100 of HSK Level 5 writing test with the *Standards*.

Table 9.4 A Summary of the Results of the Content Analysis

Item	Material	QC	CF	CC	QPT
The construct of the *Standards*	The *Standards*	√	√	√	√
The construct of HSK	*HSK Rating Criteria*		√	√	√
	HSK Test Syllabus	√	√	√	√
	HSK Test Item-Writing Manual	√	√	√	

Note: QC—quantitative criteria; CF—communicative functions; CC—communicative context; QPT—quality of produced texts.

9.2 Results for Research Question Two

Research Question 2 explores the content alignment between Items 99 and 100 of HSK Level 5 writing test and the *Standards*.

Both quantitative and qualitative methods were used to answer this research question. As a quantitative research method, an online questionnaire (Questionnaire 1) was made for experts to judge the extent to which the content of Items 99 and 100 could be aligned with the *Standards*. Specifically, Items 99 and 100 of 3 sets of HSK Level 5 sample test papers were selected to be aligned with 6 selected descriptors in the *Standards* from the content perspective. Totally, 6 writing tasks (Tasks 1 – 6) needed to be judged in relation to the 6 descriptors (Descriptors 1 – 6). The research instruments, materials to be judged, and participants have already been introduced in Chapter Eight. As a qualitative research method, interviews were held to further explore the results shown by Questionnaire 1.

9.2.1 Results of the Quantitative Analysis

In terms of the content alignment between Item 99 and the *Standards*, experts' judgment on items 1 – 6, 13 – 18, 25 – 30 of the online questionnaire (Questionnaire 1) should be analyzed. Items 1 – 6 focused on the alignment between Task 1 and 6 descriptors. Items 13 – 18 highlighted the alignment between Task 3 and 6 descriptors. Items 25 – 30 aimed at discovering the alignment between Task 5 and 6 descriptors. Those 3 writing tasks (Tasks 1, 3 and 5) were the Item 99 selected from 3 sets of HSK Level 5 sample test paper. Totally, 55 experts answered Questionnaire 1.

Firstly, a descriptive analysis was employed. Table 9.5 presents the minimum options, maximum options, means, standard deviations, skewness levels and kurtosis levels. The maximum option of each item is 5. But for half of those items, the minimum option is 1. For the other half of items, the minimum option is 2. As observed in Table 9.5, the minimum option of items aiming at exploring the alignment between item 99 and Descriptors 3, 4 and 6 is 1, which indicates a lower degree of content alignment between item 99 and those 3 descriptors. While the minimum option of items aiming at exploring the alignment between Item 99 and Descriptors 1, 2, or 5 indicate a higher degree of content alignment.

The mean of most items is close to 4, which suggests a relatively high degree of content alignment. But the mean of items which are designed to align Item 99 with Descriptor 4 is lower than those of other items.

The distribution of the questionnaire data is stable and reasonable. Because the standard deviations are small, and the levels of skewness and kurtosis are between −1 and 1.2.

Table 9.5 Descriptive Statistics of Experts' Judgment on Item 99 ($n=55$)

Task	Item	Descriptor	Minimum Statistic	Maximum Statistic	Mean Statistic	Std. Deviation Statistic	Skewness Statistic	Kurtosis Statistic
1	1	1	2	5	3.64	0.825	−0.044	−0.489
	2	2	2	5	3.56	0.938	−0.121	−0.807
	3	3	1	5	3.36	1.128	−0.289	−0.671
	4	4	1	5	3.29	1.212	−0.330	−0.807
	5	5	2	5	3.78	0.832	−0.166	−0.545
	6	6	1	5	3.58	1.031	−0.438	−0.108
3	13	1	2	5	3.71	0.786	−0.378	−0.050
	14	2	2	5	3.64	0.825	−0.250	−0.342
	15	3	1	5	3.51	0.920	−0.323	−0.063
	16	4	1	5	3.38	1.147	−0.579	−0.287
	17	5	2	5	3.76	0.793	−0.471	0.071
	18	6	1	5	3.64	0.910	−0.881	1.208
5	25	1	2	5	3.69	0.920	−0.221	−0.717
	26	2	2	5	3.65	0.907	−0.326	−0.580
	27	3	1	5	3.60	0.955	−0.430	−0.126
	28	4	1	5	3.44	1.118	−0.700	0.053
	29	5	2	5	3.73	0.870	−0.303	−0.467
	30	6	1	5	3.67	0.924	−0.896	1.185

Then, a binomial test was adopted to further analyze the distribution of the questionnaire data. All items in Questionnaire 1 are in the form of Likert five-point scales. The five numerical options are divided into two categories: the approval category and the disapproval category. Options 1, 2 and 3 refer to "totally untrue" "hardly true" and "basically true". Those three options belong to the disapproval category. Options 4 and 5 stand for "largely true" and "totally true". They participate in the approval category. In Table 9.6,

Group 1 (category≤3) represents the disapproval category, while Group 2 (category>3) represents the approval category.

Since the test proportion is 0.6, the hypothesis of the present research is that if the observed proportions of Group 1 are mostly greater than 0.4, then most experts disagree that Item 99 can be aligned with the *Standards* from the content perspective. As shown in Table 9.6, most observed proportions of Group 1 are ≤ 0.4, and the value of p is mostly lower than 0.05, which implies that there exists a significant difference between Groups 1 and 2. Hence, the hypopresent research is refuted. Besides, the number of the experts in Group 2 is bigger than that in Group 1. To sum up, according to the results of the binomial test, most experts think that Item 99 can be aligned with the *Standards* from the content perspective.

Table 9.6　Binomial Test of Experts' Judgment on Item 99

Item	Group	N	Observed Prop.	Test Prop.	Exact Sig. (1-tailed)
1	Group 1	24	0.4	0.6	0.010[a]
	Group 2	31	0.6		
	Total	55	1.0		
2	Group 1	25	0.5	0.6	0.020[a]
	Group 2	30	0.5		
	Total	55	1.0		
3	Group 1	28	0.5	0.6	0.108[a]
	Group 2	27	0.5		
	Total	55	1.0		
4	Group 1	28	0.5	0.6	0.108[a]
	Group 2	27	0.5		
	Total	55	1.0		
5	Group 1	20	0.4	0.6	0.000[a]
	Group 2	35	0.6		
	Total	55	1.0		

continued

Item	Group	N	Observed Prop.	Test Prop.	Exact Sig. (1-tailed)
6	Group 1	25	0.5	0.6	0.020[a]
	Group 2	30	0.5		
	Total	55	1.0		
13	Group 1	19	0.3	0.6	0.000[a]
	Group 2	36	0.7		
	Total	55	1.0		
14	Group 1	22	0.4	0.6	0.002[a]
	Group 2	33	0.6		
	Total	55	1.0		
15	Group 1	26	0.5	0.6	0.038[a]
	Group 2	29	0.5		
	Total	55	1.0		
16	Group 1	26	0.5	0.6	0.038[a]
	Group 2	29	0.5		
	Total	55	1.0		
17	Group 1	17	0.3	0.6	0.000[a]
	Group 2	38	0.7		
	Total	55	1.0		
18	Group 1	20	0.4	0.6	0.000[a]
	Group 2	35	0.6		
	Total	55	1.0		
25	Group 1	22	0.4	0.6	0.002[a]
	Group 2	33	0.6		
	Total	55	1.0		
26	Group 1	21	0.4	0.6	0.001[a]
	Group 2	34	0.6		
	Total	55	1.0		

continued

Item	Group	N	Observed Prop.	Test Prop.	Exact Sig. (1-tailed)
27	Group 1	23	0.4	0.6	0.005[a]
	Group 2	32	0.6		
	Total	55	1.0		
28	Group 1	25	0.5	0.6	0.020[a]
	Group 2	30	0.5		
	Total	55	1.0		
29	Group 1	20	0.4	0.6	0.000[a]
	Group 2	35	0.6		
	Total	55	1.0		
30	Group 1	19	0.3	0.6	0.000[a]
	Group 2	36	0.7		
	Total	55	1.0		

Note: Alternative hypopresent research states that the proportion of cases in the first group<0.6.

Next, one-way ANOVA was used to further explore the relation between Item 99 and each of the six descriptors. As t-test is usually used to analyze whether there is a significant difference between the means of two samples, while one-way ANOVA is applicable for the comparison among the means of three or more samples (Woods et al., 2000).

From Table 9.7, the value of p is $0.004 < 0.01$, which confirms that a significant difference among experts' judgment on Descriptors 1, 2, 3, 4, 5, and 6 does exist. However, the results of the one-way ANOVA cannot reflect which specific pair of means differ from each other (Li, 2001).

Table 9.7　Differences among Experts' Judgment on Each Descriptor

	Sum of Squares	df	Mean Square	F	Sig.
Between Groups	15.961	5	3.192	3.532	0.004
Within Groups	889.358	984	0.904		
Total	905.318	989			

Therefore, a post-hoc test was then used to make multiple comparisons among experts' judgment on each descriptor. According to Table 9.8, experts' judgment on Descriptor 4 and their judgment on Descriptors 1, 2, 5 and 6 are significantly different. As illustrated in the fifth column of Table 9.8, the value of p is always lower than 0.05, which indicates a significant difference. Similarly, a significant difference at the 0.05 level exists between the judgment on Descriptor 3, and the judgment on Descriptor 5, because the value of p is 0.011<0.05.

Furthermore, the degree of the alignment between Item 99 and Descriptor 4 is lower than the degree of the alignment between Item 99 and Descriptors 1, 2, 5 and 6 as the values shown in the third column of Table 9.8 are negative. In a word, the alignment between Item 99 and Descriptor 4 is relatively unsatisfactory. By the same token, the degree of the alignment between Item 99 and Descriptor 3 is lower than the degree of the alignment between Item 99 and Descriptor 5, shown by the value of the mean difference which is negative.

Table 9.8 Multiple Comparisons between the Alignment on Each Descriptor

(I) Descriptor	(J) Descriptor	Mean Difference (I−J)	Std. Error	Sig.	95% Confidence Interval	
					Lower Bound	Upper Bound
1	2	0.060 61	0.104 67	0.563	−0.144 8	0.266 0
	3	0.187 88	0.104 67	0.073	−0.017 5	0.393 3
	4	0.309 09*	0.104 67	0.003	0.103 7	0.514 5
	5	−0.078 79	0.104 67	0.452	−0.284 2	0.126 6
	6	0.048 48	0.104 67	0.643	−0.156 9	0.253 9
2	1	−0.060 61	0.104 67	0.563	−0.266 0	0.144 8
	3	0.127 27	0.104 67	0.224	−0.078 1	0.332 7
	4	0.248 48*	0.104 67	0.018	0.043 1	0.453 9
	5	−0.139 39	0.104 67	0.183	−0.344 8	0.066 0
	6	−0.012 12	0.104 67	0.908	−0.217 5	0.193 3

continued

(I) Descriptor	(J) Descriptor	Mean Difference (I-J)	Std. Error	Sig.	95% Confidence Interval	
					Lower Bound	Upper Bound
3	1	−0.187 88	0.104 67	0.073	−0.393 3	0.017 5
	2	−0.127 27	0.104 67	0.224	−0.332 7	0.078 1
	4	0.121 21	0.104 67	0.247	−0.084 2	0.326 6
	5	−0.266 67*	0.104 67	0.011	−0.472 1	−0.061 3
	6	−0.139 39	0.104 67	0.183	−0.344 8	0.066 0
4	1	−0.309 09*	0.104 67	0.003	−0.514 5	−0.103 7
	2	−0.248 48*	0.104 67	0.018	−0.453 9	−0.043 1
	3	−0.121 21	0.104 67	0.247	−0.326 6	0.084 2
	5	−0.387 88*	0.104 67	0.000	−0.593 3	−0.182 5
	6	−0.260 61*	0.104 67	0.013	−0.466 0	−0.055 2
5	1	0.078 79	0.104 67	0.452	−0.126 6	0.284 2
	2	0.139 39	0.104 67	0.183	−0.066 0	0.344 8
	3	0.266 67*	0.104 67	0.011	0.061 3	0.472 1
	4	0.387 88*	0.104 67	0.000	0.182 5	0.593 3
	6	0.127 27	0.104 67	0.224	−0.078 1	0.332 7
6	1	−0.048 48	0.104 67	0.643	−0.253 9	0.156 9
	2	0.012 12	0.104 67	0.908	−0.193 3	0.217 5
	3	0.139 39	0.104 67	0.183	−0.066 0	0.344 8
	4	0.260 61*	0.104 67	0.013	0.055 2	0.466 0
	5	−0.127 27	0.104 67	0.224	−0.332 7	0.078 1

*. The mean difference is significant at the 0.05 level.

In terms of the content alignment between Item 100 and the *Standards*, the experts' judgment on items 7 – 12, 19 – 24, 31 – 36 of the online questionnaire (Questionnaire 1) should be analyzed. Items 7 – 12 focus on the alignment between Task 2 and 6 descriptors. Items 19 – 24 highlight the alignment between Task 4 and 6 descriptors. Items 31 – 36 aim at discovering the alignment between Task 6 and 6 descriptors. Those 3 writing tasks (Task 2, 4 and 6) are the Item 100 selected from 3 sets of HSK Level 5 sample test papers. In total, 55 experts answered Questionnaire 1.

Firstly, a descriptive analysis was adopted. According to Table 9.9, the maximum option of each item is 5, and the minimum option of most items is 1. Based on the sixth column of Table 9.9, the mean of all items is greater than 3 and over half of them are close to 4. It indicates a relatively satisfactory alignment. What is noteworthy is that the mean of items designed to align Item 100 with Descriptor 3 is always lower than that of other items, which suggests a relatively low degree of content alignment. The questionnaire data is stable and distributed in an acceptable range, because the values of skewness and kurtosis are in the range of -1 and 1, and the standard deviations are relatively small.

Table 9.9 Descriptive Statistics of Experts' Judgment on Item 100 ($n=55$)

Task	Item	Descriptor	Minimum	Maximum	Mean	Std. Deviation	Skewness	Kurtosis
			Statistic	Statistic	Statistic	Statistic	Statistic	Statistic
2	7	1	2	5	3.49	0.900	-0.209	-0.710
	8	2	1	5	3.42	0.937	-0.245	-0.295
	9	3	1	5	3.20	1.043	-0.114	-0.378
	10	4	1	5	3.49	1.153	-0.843	-0.056
	11	5	1	5	3.55	0.899	-0.538	0.172
	12	6	1	5	3.49	0.998	-0.787	0.460
4	19	1	2	5	3.62	0.933	-0.287	-0.707
	20	2	1	5	3.60	0.993	-0.524	-0.298
	21	3	1	5	3.45	0.978	-0.423	0.041
	22	4	1	5	3.47	1.260	-0.628	-0.546
	23	5	1	5	3.78	0.896	-0.828	0.879
	24	6	1	5	3.55	0.978	-0.933	0.856
6	31	1	2	5	3.71	0.896	-0.663	-0.196
	32	2	2	5	3.65	0.865	-0.321	-0.432
	33	3	1	5	3.38	1.063	-0.543	-0.346
	34	4	1	5	3.53	1.200	-0.868	-0.020
	35	5	1	5	3.64	0.988	-0.634	0.362
	36	6	1	5	3.62	1.027	-0.863	0.611

Then, a binomial test was adopted to further discuss the distribution of the questionnaire data. Table 9.10 illustrates the results of the binomial test of experts' judgment on Item 100. The five options of the questionnaire represent five degrees of content alignment and are divided into two categories: the approval and disapproval categories. In Table 9.10, Group 1 refers to the disapproval category and Group 2 stands for the approval category. Options 1, 2 and 3 belong to Group 1. Options 4 and 5 belong to Group 2. Considering the test proportion, the hypopresent research is that if the observed proportion of Group 1 is mostly greater than 0.4, then most experts think that Item 100 can't be aligned with the *Standards* from the content perspective.

As illustrated in Table 9.10, the observed proportion of Group 1 is mostly $\leqslant 0.4$, and the value of p is mostly lower than 0.05. Thus, the hypopresent research is refuted. Besides, There are much more experts in Group 2 than in Group 1. In summary, most experts think that Item 100 can be aligned with the *Standards* from the content perspective.

Table 9.10 Binomial Test of Experts' Judgment on Item 100

Item	Group	N	Observed Prop.	Test Prop.	Exact Sig. (1-tailed)
7	Group 1	25	0.5	0.6	0.020[a]
	Group 2	30	0.5		
	Total	55	1.0		
8	Group 1	28	0.5	0.6	0.108[a]
	Group 2	27	0.5		
	Total	55	1.0		
9	Group 1	34	0.6	0.6	0.449
	Group 2	21	0.4		
	Total	55	1.0		

continued

Item	Group	N	Observed Prop.	Test Prop.	Exact Sig. (1-tailed)
10	Group 1	20	0.4	0.6	0.000[a]
	Group 2	35	0.6		
	Total	55	1.0		
11	Group 1	23	0.4	0.6	0.005[a]
	Group 2	32	0.6		
	Total	55	1.0		
12	Group 1	23	0.4	0.6	0.005[a]
	Group 2	32	0.6		
	Total	55	1.0		
19	Group 1	22	0.4	0.6	0.002[a]
	Group 2	33	0.6		
	Total	55	1.0		
20	Group 1	21	0.4	0.6	0.001[a]
	Group 2	34	0.6		
	Total	55	1.0		
21	Group 1	27	0.5	0.6	0.066[a]
	Group 2	28	0.5		
	Total	55	1.0		
22	Group 1	23	0.4	0.6	0.005[a]
	Group 2	32	0.6		
	Total	55	1.0		
23	Group 1	16	0.3	0.6	0.000[a]
	Group 2	39	0.7		
	Total	55	1.0		
24	Group 1	21	0.4	0.6	0.001[a]
	Group 2	34	0.6		
	Total	55	1.0		

continued

Item	Group	N	Observed Prop.	Test Prop.	Exact Sig. (1-tailed)
31	Group 1	16	0.3	0.6	0.000[a]
	Group 2	39	0.7		
	Total	55	1.0		
32	Group 1	21	0.4	0.6	0.001[a]
	Group 2	34	0.6		
	Total	55	1.0		
33	Group 1	25	0.5	0.6	0.020[a]
	Group 2	30	0.5		
	Total	55	1.0		
34	Group 1	20	0.4	0.6	0.000[a]
	Group 2	35	0.6		
	Total	55	1.0		
35	Group 1	22	0.4	0.6	0.002[a]
	Group 2	33	0.6		
	Total	55	1.0		
36	Group 1	20	0.4	0.6	0.000[a]
	Group 2	35	0.6		
	Total	55	1.0		

note: Alternative hypopresent research states that the proportion of cases in the first group <0.6.

Table 9.11 Differences among Experts' Judgment on Each Descriptor

	Sum of Squares	df	Mean Square	F	Sig.
Between Groups	9.487	5	1.897	1.884	0.094
Within Groups	990.776	984	1.007		
Total	1000.263	989			

To dig out the relation between Item 100 and each of the six descriptors, the researcher made a one-way ANOVA test. According to Table 9.11, the value of p is $0.094 > 0.05$. There is no significant difference among experts' judgment on each of the six descriptors. However, there is still a need to make multiple comparisons.

According to Table 9.12, the experts' judgment on Descriptor 3 is significantly different from their judgment on Descriptors 1 and 5 at the level of 0.05, because the values of p are 0.019 and 0.005, both of which are lower than 0.05.

Furthermore, the degree of alignment between Item 100 and Descriptor 3 is lower than the degree of alignment between Item 100 and Descriptor 1, as well as the degree of alignment between Item 100 and Descriptor 5. In a word, the content alignment between Item 100 and Descriptor 3 is relatively unsatisfactory.

Table 9.12 Multiple Comparisons between the Alignment on Each Descriptor

(I) Descriptor	(J) Descriptor	Mean Difference (I-J)	Std. Error	Sig.	95% Confidence Interval	
					Lower Bound	Upper Bound
1	2	0.048 48	0.110 47	0.661	−0.168 3	0.265 3
	3	0.260 61*	0.110 47	0.019	0.043 8	0.477 4
	4	0.109 09	0.110 47	0.324	−0.107 7	0.325 9
	5	−0.048 48	0.110 47	0.661	−0.265 3	0.168 3
	6	0.054 55	0.110 47	0.622	−0.162 2	0.271 3
2	1	−0.048 48	0.110 47	0.661	−0.265 3	0.168 3
	3	0.212 12	0.110 47	0.055	−0.004 7	0.428 9
	4	0.060 61	0.110 47	0.583	−0.156 2	0.277 4
	5	−0.096 97	0.110 47	0.380	−0.313 8	0.119 8
	6	0.006 06	0.110 47	0.956	−0.210 7	0.222 9
3	1	−0.260 61*	0.110 47	0.019	−0.477 4	−0.043 8
	2	−0.212 12	0.110 47	0.055	−0.428 9	0.004 7
	4	−0.151 52	0.110 47	0.171	−0.368 3	0.065 3
	5	−0.309 09*	0.110 47	0.005	−0.525 9	−0.092 3
	6	−0.206 06	0.110 47	0.062	−0.422 9	0.010 7

continued

(I) Descriptor	(J) Descriptor	Mean Difference (I-J)	Std. Error	Sig.	95% Confidence Interval	
					Lower Bound	Upper Bound
4	1	−0.109 09	0.110 47	0.324	−0.325 9	0.107 7
	2	−0.060 61	0.110 47	0.583	−0.277 4	0.156 2
	3	0.151 52	0.110 47	0.171	−0.065 3	0.368 3
	5	−0.157 58	0.110 47	0.154	−0.374 4	0.059 2
	6	−0.054 55	0.110 47	0.622	−0.271 3	0.162 2
5	1	0.048 48	0.110 47	0.661	−0.168 3	0.265 3
	2	0.096 97	0.110 47	0.380	−0.119 8	0.313 8
	3	0.309 09*	0.110 47	0.005	0.092 3	0.525 9
	4	0.157 58	0.110 47	0.154	−0.059 2	0.374 4
	6	0.103 03	0.110 47	0.351	−0.113 8	0.319 8
6	1	−0.054 55	0.110 47	0.622	−0.271 3	0.162 2
	2	−0.006 06	0.110 47	0.956	−0.222 9	0.210 7
	3	0.206 06	0.110 47	0.062	−0.010 7	0.422 9
	4	0.054 55	0.110 47	0.622	−0.162 2	0.271 3
	5	−0.103 03	0.110 47	0.351	−0.319 8	0.113 8

*. The mean difference is significant at the 0.05 level.

9.2.2 Results of the Qualitative Analysis

Totally, 4 experts (Interviewees A, B, C and D) who had answered Questionnaire 1 were invited to have an interview. Interviewees A and B made comments, and gave a general description of the content alignment between Item 99 and the *Standards*. Interviewees C and D had an interview about the content alignment between Item 100 and the *Standards*.

In terms of the content alignment between Item 99 and the *Standards*, both Interviewees A and B mentioned that three tasks (Tasks 1, 3 and 5) can be aligned with the *Standards* basically, which corroborates the results of the quantitative analysis. However, descriptors are more informative in describing candidates' knowledge of Chinese characters, words and phrases, as well as in describing the quality of candidates' scripts, especially the text genres and topics.

Because of the lack of candidates' scripts, the words provided in Item 99 and the instructions of Item 99 serve as important references for experts to make the judgment. However, limited information can be obtained from the instructions. Both experts pointed out that the directions of Item 99 should be enriched in order to have a higher degree of content alignment. Therefore, experts' judgment is mainly based on the words provided by Item 99. Parts of their replies are shown as follows:

Q. Do you think Item 99 can be aligned with the *Standards*? And why?

Interviewee A: Basically, I think Item 99 can be aligned with Descriptors 1, 2, 3, 4 and 5, by analyzing the words provided by Item 99. But when it comes to the alignment between Item 99 and Descriptor 6, I think Item 99 doesn't examine candidates' ability to write expositions, because the words provided in Item 99 cannot show test developers' tendency to lead candidates to write an exposition. The words shown in Task 1 lead to an argumentation, while the words shown in Task 3 are usually used together in a narrative. In terms of the words provided in Task 5, they are commonly used in an article on the topic of business and commerce, so it is possible for candidates to write an exposition. Since limited information is provided by the instructions, I am not sure whether Task 5 can definitely assess candidates' ability to write an exposition.

Interviewee B: Generally speaking, Item 99 can basically cover the requirements of the *Standards*. However, descriptors are relatively informative and demanding, especially on learners' language knowledge, including their knowledge of Chinese characters, as well as words and phrases. When aligning Item 99 with Descriptors 1, 2, and 3, I focus on the complexity and difficulty of the words provided by Item 99. With no candidates' scripts and limited instructions of Item 99, I feel it difficult to link Item 99 with Descriptors 4, 5 and 6, because those 3 descriptors are concerned about candidates' ability to write an article. Mastering the provided words is a necessity for candidates to write an article, because an article always consists of a great number of words. Thus, my judgment is mainly based on the words provided by Item 99.

As for the content alignment between Item 100 and the *Standards*, both Interviewees C and D pointed out that 3 tasks (Tasks 2, 4 and 6) are basically linked to the *Standards*. However, the requirements of the *Standards* are relatively high, especially on the expected length of candidates' scripts, as well as on the rhetorical tasks. The rhetorical task, as a dimension of analyzing writing tasks, broadly refers to one of the traditional discourse modes of narration, exposition, and argument. It is usually mentioned in the instructions to test takers (Weigle, 2002). The alignment on Item 99 is better than that on Item 100, because more information is provided by Item 99.

Different from Item 99, a picture is provided by Item 100. Interviewees can get limited information from the picture and instructions. Besides, due to the lack of candidates' scripts of Item 100, interviewees feel it difficult for them to make content alignment. They make inferences mainly based on the instructions of Item 100, as well as their experience and professional knowledge. To have a better degree of content alignment, the instructions of Item 100 should be enriched. Texts of their answers are selected as follows:

Q. Do you think Item 100 can be aligned with the *Standards*? And why?

Interviewee C: Those three tasks are very similar and examine similar abilities, because they all require candidates to write a short passage of 80 Chinese characters based on the provided picture. In general, Item 100 can basically be aligned with the *Standards*. But requirements of the *Standards* are higher than those of Item 100. It seems to be urgent for us to release HSK Levels 7, 8 and 9. Item 100 can assess candidates' ability to write an article with comparatively appropriate vocabulary, basically correct sentence patterns, comparatively complete content, comparatively clear expression, and basically standard format in a limited time. But it's difficult to evaluate candidates' ability to write or use specific Chinese characters and sentence patterns. Besides, the rhetorical tasks and expected topics are not mentioned by test questions, while the text genres and topics are refined in descriptors.

Interviewee D: Overall, Item 100 can be basically linked to the *Standards* from the content perspective. But the *Standards* is relatively informative and demanding especially when describing the expected length of candidates' scripts. According to the instructions of Item 100, too little information is provided, and requirements on candidates are not clearly pointed out. The picture provided in Item 100 has nearly no influence on my judgment because candidates can write a narrative, argumentation, or exposition on different topics according to the provided picture. It means that the picture makes nearly no limitation on candidates' writing. I think the instructions of Item 100 should be enriched in terms of the expected length, rhetorical tasks, and expected topics.

9.2.3 Summary

After making both quantitative and qualitative analyses, the results of the second research question are summarized in this section. Items 99 and 100 can be basically aligned with the *Standards* Level 5 from the content perspective, which corroborates the results of the first research question, but the *Standards* is more informative. In addition, the degree of content alignment on each descriptor is different. Specifically, the content alignment between Item 99 and Descriptor 4, as well as between Item 100 and Descriptor 3 is relatively unsatisfactory.

9.3 Results for Research Question Three

Research Questions 1 and 2 explore the content alignment between HSK Level 5 writing test and the *Standards*. Then, the third question investigates HSK Level 5 test takers' self-evaluation on the extent to which they can meet the requirements of the writing sub-scales in the *Standards* Level 5. Besides, the relation between their self-evaluation and their actual HSK writing scores is also analyzed as a method of collecting evidence for the validity of examinees' self-evaluation.

Only the quantitative questionnaire survey was used to answer this problem. Specifically, examinee's evaluation of their writing ability was collected by the self-evaluation questionnaire. Items 31 to 40 in the self-evaluation questionnaire aimed at evaluating the writing ability. All those 10 questions were designed on the basis of descriptors in the *Standards*, and were in the form of Likert five-point scales. 276 examinees of HSK Level 5 answered the questionnaire. They were invited to choose a numerical option from five numerical options according to their actual situation. Options 1 to 5 standed for "totally untrue" "hardly true" "basically true" "largely true" and "totally true" respectively.

Then, the HSK scores of those examinees were searched by their candidate numbers entered in the self-evaluation questionnaire. However, 80 of them did not provide the correct candidate numbers. Therefore, the questionnaire data from only 196 examinees was used to answer the third research question.

9.3.1 Results of Examinees' Self-Evaluation

A descriptive analysis of the self-evaluation questionnaire data was first adopted. Table 9.13 illustrates the minimum options, maximum options, means, standard deviations, as well as levels of skewness and kurtosis. The minimum option of items 31 – 40 is 1, and the maximum option is 5 always. Standard deviations are around 1. Since the value of skewness and kurtosis ranges from −1 to 1, the questionnaire data is normally distributed. The mean of most items is larger than 3, which suggests that examinees think that they can meet the requirements of the *Standards* Level 5.

Table 9.13 Descriptive Statistics of Examinees' Self-Evaluation ($n=276$)

Item	Minimum	Maximum	Mean	Std. Deviation	Skewness		Kurtosis	
	Statistic	Statistic	Statistic	Statistic	Statistic	Std. Error	Statistic	Std. Error
31	1	5	3.30	1.006	−0.156	0.147	−0.379	0.292
32	1	5	2.98	1.056	0.036	0.147	−0.612	0.292
33	1	5	3.04	0.986	−0.019	0.147	−0.433	0.292
34	1	5	3.07	1.012	−0.118	0.147	−0.369	0.292
35	1	5	3.05	1.038	0.009	0.147	−0.485	0.292
36	1	5	3.05	1.013	0.081	0.147	−0.502	0.292
37	1	5	3.05	1.024	0.049	0.147	−0.578	0.292
38	1	5	3.10	0.971	0.059	0.147	−0.372	0.292
39	1	5	3.08	1.068	−0.026	0.147	−0.541	0.292
40	1	5	2.91	1.098	0.039	0.147	−0.707	0.292

To explore the validity of examinees' self-evaluation, those examinees' HSK scores were searched by the Center for Language Education and Cooperation. Although 276 examinees answered the questionnaire in total, HSK scores of only 196 examinees were found. The present study only focused on Items 99 and 100 of HSK Level 5 writing test. Candidates' scripts of Items 99 and 100 were scored out of 21 points.

9.3.2 The Relation between Examinees' Self-Evaluation and Their Overall Scores of Items 99 and 100

Both Item 99 and Item 100 were scored out of 21 points. Combining scores on those two questions, the researcher analyzed the relation between examinees' overall scores on those two questions and their self-evaluation of their writing ability.

First, a scatter diagram was drawn to show the tendency of the two groups of data. As illustrated in Figure 9.1, there seems to be no linear relation between the overall scores and questionnaire options. Then, in terms of the results of a correlation analysis shown in Table 9.14, the value of p is larger than 0.05. Possibly there is no significant correlation between examinees' self-evaluation and their overall scores.

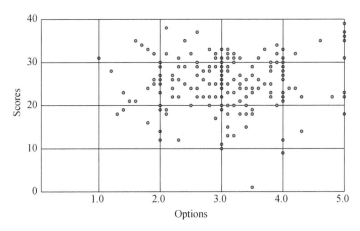

Figure 9.1 Scatter Diagram of Overall Scores and Questionnaire Options ($n=196$)

Table 9.14 Correlations between Overall Scores and Questionnaire Options ($n=196$)

		Overall scores	Questionnaire options
Overall scores	Pearson Correlation	1	0.109
	Sig. (2-tailed)		0.129
	n	196	196
Questionnaire options	Pearson Correlation	0.109	1
	Sig. (2-tailed)	0.129	
	n	196	196

To have a further exploration, based on their overall scores of Items 99 and 100, the researcher divided the 196 candidates into 2 groups: Group 1 and Group 2. Group 1 referred to the low-score group, while Group 2 stood for the high-score group.

47 candidates belonged to the first group, and their overall scores were lower than or equal to 21. As observed in Figure 9.2, no linear relation between 47 candidates' overall scores and their questionnaire options seems to exist. It is then ensured that no significant difference exists as the sig value shown in Table 9.15 is 0.462>0.05.

In Group 2 or the high-score group, there were 149 candidates whose overall scores were higher than 21. First, a scatter diagram was made to

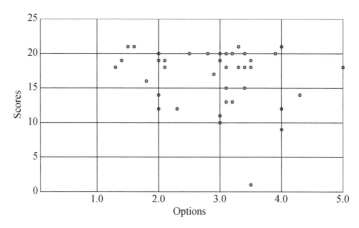

Figure 9.2　Scatter Diagram of Overall Scores and Questionnaire Options ($n=47$)

Table 9.15　Correlations between Overall Scores and Questionnaire Options ($n=47$)

		Overall scores	Questionnaire options
Overall scores	Pearson Correlation	1	−0.110
	Sig. (2-tailed)		0.462
	n	47	47
Questionnaire options	Pearson Correlation	−0.110	1
	Sig. (2-tailed)	0.462	
	n	47	47

discover the relation between 149 candidates' overall scores and their questionnaire options. As shown in Figure 9.3, there seems to be no linear relation. According to Table 9.16, the value of p indicates that there exists no significant relation with a value of 0.169.

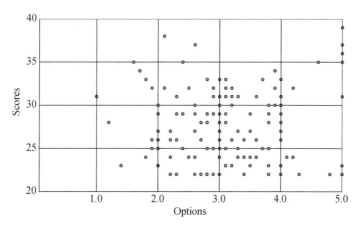

Figure 9.3   Scatter Diagram of Overall Scores and Questionnaire Options ($n=149$)

Table 9.16   Correlations between Overall Scores and Questionnaire Options ($n=149$)

		Overall scores	Questionnaire options
Overall scores	Pearson Correlation	1	0.113
	Sig. (2-tailed)		0.169
	n	149	149
Questionnaire options	Pearson Correlation	0.113	1
	Sig. (2-tailed)	0.169	
	n	149	149

According to their questionnaire options, 196 candidates were classified into two groups again: Group 1 and Group 2. This time, candidates in Group 1 were those who didn't think they could reach the requirements of the Standards Level 5. The mean of their questionnaire options was less than or equalled 3. Candidates involved in Group 2 were those who considered that they could reach the requirements of the *Standards* Level 5. The mean of their questionnaire options was higher than 3.

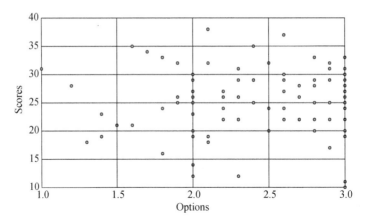

Figure 9.4 Scatter Diagram of Overall Scores and Questionnaire Options ($n=97$)

Table 9.17 Correlations between Overall Scores and Questionnaire Options ($n=97$)

		Overall scores	Questionnaire options
Overall scores	Pearson Correlation	1	0.021
	Sig. (2-tailed)		0.835
	n	97	97
Questionnaire options	Pearson Correlation	0.021	1
	Sig. (2-tailed)	0.835	
	n	97	97

Totally, 97 candidates belonged to Group 1. A scatter diagram was drawn before the correlation analysis. According to Figure 9.4, there is no linear relation between the overall scores of those 97 candidates and their questionnaire options. Table 9.17 further presents that no significant correlation exists, because the value of p is 0.835>0.05.

In Group 2, there were 99 candidates. As observed in Figure 9.5, the scatter of their overall scores and questionnaire options rises from the lower left corner to the top of the right-hand corner generally, which suggests that there may exist a positive linear relation.

Table 9.18 illustrates that the value of p is 0.002, which is less than 0.01. It indicates a significant correlation between their overall scores and questionnaire options at the level of 0.01, which leads to a further regression analysis.

A regression analysis was adopted to explore whether the questionnaire options of candidates in Group 2 could predict their overall scores on Items 99 and 100. In this case, candidates' overall scores should be set as the dependent variable, and their questionnaire options as the independent variable.

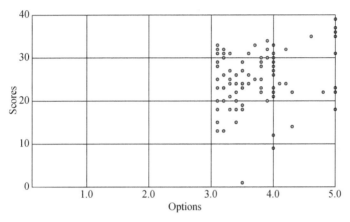

Figure 9.5 Scatter Diagram of Overall Scores and Questionnaire Options ($n=99$)

Table 9.18 Correlations between Overall Scores and Questionnaire Options ($n=99$)

		Overall scores	Questionnaire options
Overall scores	Pearson Correlation	1	0.303**
	Sig. (2-tailed)		0.002
	n	99	99
Questionnaire options	Pearson Correlation	0.303**	1
	Sig. (2-tailed)	0.002	
	n	99	99

**. Correlation is significant at the 0.01 level (2-tailed).

Table 9.19 presents the summary of Model 1 (using candidates' questionnaire options to predict their overall scores) with the coefficient of R Square of 0.092. The coefficient of R Square is usually regarded as an important indicator for judging the fit of a linear equation, and it can also reflect the predictive power of the regression model. The closer a coefficient of R Square is to 1, the better a linear regression model is.

As observed in Table 9.20, the value of p is 0.002<0.01, which means that the linear regression model or Model 1 has statistical significance.

Table 9.19 Model Summary of Model 1

Model	R	R Square	Adjusted R Square	Std. Error of the Estimate
1	0.303[a]	0.092	0.082	6.412

Predictors: (Constant), options.

Table 9.20 ANOVA Analysis of Model 1

Model		Sum of Squares	df	Mean Square	F	Sig.
1	Regression	403.386	1	403.386	9.811	0.002[b]
	Residual	3 988.251	97	41.116		
	Total	4 391.636	98			

Predictors: (Constant), options.

As illustrated in Table 9.21, the value of p is 0.002<0.01. Thus, the test of the coefficient is statistically significant, which means that candidates' questionnaire options can largely predict their overall scores. The ability of Model 1 to explain the variation of overall scores is shown by the value of R Square reported before. The regression equation may be concluded as: $y=11.768+3.549x$. In this equation, "x" refers to candidates' questionnaire options, and "y" refers to their overall scores.

Table 9.21 Coefficients of Model 1

Model 1	Unstandardized Coefficients		Standardized Coefficients	t	Sig.
	B	Std. Error	Beta		
(Constant)	11.768	4.359		2.700	0.008
options	3.549	1.133	0.303	3.132	0.002

Dependent Variable: scores

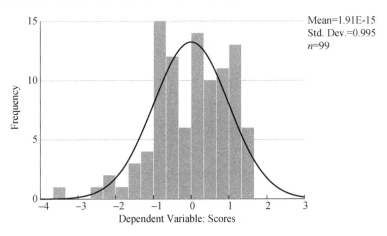

Figure 9.6 Histogram of Regression Standardized Residual in Model 1

The histogram of regression standardized residual shown in Figure 9.6 indicates the left and right sides are generally symmetric. As shown in Figure 9.7, points are roughly scattered on the oblique line. The normality of residual is not the most optimal, but it can be accepted. Therefore, the regression equation of Model 1 passes the test of the normality of standardized residual.

Then, to discover whether their overall scores can predict their questionnaire options, a further analysis taking candidates' questionnaire options as the dependent variable, and their overall scores on Items 99 and 100 as the independent variable was conducted.

In Table 9.22, Model 2 means using candidates' overall scores to predict their questionnaire options. It can be observed from Table 9.22 that the coefficient of R Square is 0.092, which indicates the predictive power of candidates' overall scores.

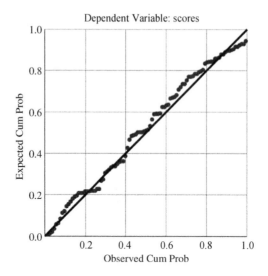

Figure 9.7 Normal P-P Plot of Regression Standardized Residual in Model 1
Dependent Variable: scores

Table 9.22 Model Summary of Model 2

Model	R	R Square	Adjusted R Square	Std. Error of the Estimate
2	0.303[a]	0.092	0.082	0.5476

Predictors: (Constant), scores. Dependent Variable: options.

As illustrated in the last column of Table 9.23, the value of p is 0.002 < 0.01. Thus, there is a significant correlation between candidates' overall scores and their questionnaire options, and the linear regression model or Model 2 has a statistical significance.

Besides, as shown in Table 9.24, the sig value is 0.002 < 0.01. It means that the test of coefficient of Model 2 is of statistical significance. In conclusion, candidates' overall scores on Items 99 and 100 have a predict power (R Square = 0.092) to their questionnaire options. The regression equation of Model 2 may be expressed as: $y = 3.151 + 0.026x$. In this equation, "x" refers to candidates' overall scores, and "y" refers to their questionnaire options.

Table 9.23 ANOVA Analysis of Model 2

Model		Sum of Squares	df	Mean Square	F	Sig.
2	Regression	2.942	1	2.932	9.811	0.002[b]
	Residual	29.086	97	0.300		
	Total	32.027	98			

Predictors: (Constant), scores. Dependent Variable: options.

Table 9.24 Coefficients of Model 2

Model		Unstandardized Coefficients		Standardized Coefficients	t	Sig.
		B	Std. Error	Beta		
2	(Constant)	3.151	0.216		14.590	0.000
	Scores	0.026	0.008	0.303	3.132	0.002

Dependent Variable: options.

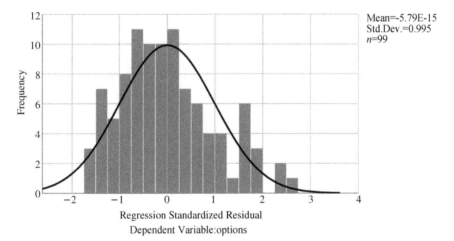

Figure 9.8 Histogram of Regression Standardized Residual in Model 2

From Figure 9.8, it can be observed that the left and right sides are generally symmetric. As shown in Figure 9.9, points are roughly scattered on the oblique line. The normality of residual is not the most optimal, but it can be accepted. Hence, the regression equation of Model 2 passes the test of the normality of standardized residual.

In summary, a significant positive linear relation can only be found between the questionnaire options of 99 examinees who think they can reach

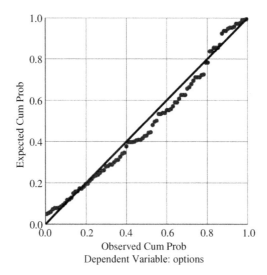

Figure 9.9 Normal P-P Plot of Regression Standardized Residual in Model 2

the requirements of the *Standards* Level 5 and their overall scores on Items 99 and 100. In other words, those 99 examinees think that they can reach the requirements of the *Standards* Level 5 and their self-evaluation data is reliable.

Since a decision is usually made on the cut-off score of the borderline performance in the step of standard setting, a cut-off score will be given based on those 99 examinees' self-evaluation. The cut-off score will be used to explain whether an examinee of HSK Level 5 can reach the requirements of the *Standards* Level 5, and to differentiate examinees of HSK Level 5 into two proficiency levels: Level 5 or Level 5 minus.

According to those 99 candidates' self-evaluation, a group of borderline candidates were selected, and the mean of their self-evaluation was the lowest among those 99 examinees. Table 9.25 presents the mean of their questionnaire options and the overall scores on Items 99 and 100 of those borderline candidates. There are 12 borderline examinees. The average overall score of those 12 examinees is regarded as the cut-off score. Therefore, the cut-off score is 23.75. Examinees whose overall scores of Items 99 and 100 are higher than or equal to 23.75 can be allocated to the *Standards* Level 5.

Table 9.25 A Description of Borderline Examinees

Examinee	The mean of their questionnaire options	Overall scores on Items 99 and 100
1	3.1	29
2	3.1	28
3	3.1	33
4	3.1	13
5	3.1	20
6	3.1	18
7	3.1	32
8	3.1	18
9	3.1	31
10	3.1	25
11	3.1	15
12	3.1	23

9.3.3 The Relation between Examinees' Self-Evaluation and Their Scores on Item 99

A correlation analysis was applied to explore the relation between candidates' scores on Item 99 and their questionnaire options. First, a scatter diagram was made. According to Figure 9.10, the distribution of those two

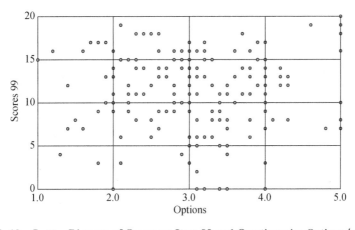

Figure 9.10 Scatter Diagram of Scores on Item 99 and Questionnaire Options ($n=196$)

groups of data shows no linear relation. Table 9.26 further illustrates that there is no significant correlation between candidates' scores on Item 99 and their questionnaire options, because the value of p is 0.204>0.05.

Table 9.26　Correlations between Scores on Item 99 and Questionnaire Options ($n=196$)

		Scores on Item 99	Questionnaire options
Scores on Item 99	Pearson Correlation	1	0.091
	Sig. (2-tailed)		0.204
	n	196	196
Questionnaire options	Pearson Correlation	0.091	1
	Sig. (2-tailed)	0.204	
	n	196	196

To have a further exploration, according to their actual scores on Item 99, the researchers divided examinees into two groups: Group 1 and Group 2. Group 1 referred to the low-score group, while Group 2 referred to the high-score group.

Totally, 77 candidates belonged to Group 1. Their scores on Item 99 were lower than 11. Similarly, a scatter diagram was drawn as well. As observed in Figure 9.11, no linear relation can be detected.

The Pearson correlation analysis was then applied to further represent the relation between the two groups of data. As shown in Table 9.27, the value of p is 0.906, which possibly reflects that no significant correlation exists.

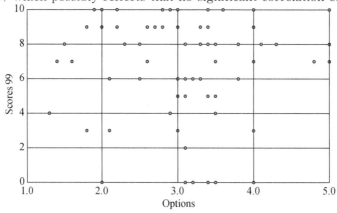

Figure 9.11　Scatter Diagram of Scores on Item 99 and Questionnaire Options ($n=77$)

Table 9.27 Correlations between Scores on Item 99 and Questionnaire Options (*n*=77)

		Scores on Item 99	Questionnaire options
Scores on Item 99	Pearson Correlation	1	0.014
	Sig. (2-tailed)		0.906
	n	77	77
Questionnaire options	Pearson Correlation	0.014	1
	Sig. (2-tailed)	0.906	
	n	77	77

The scores on Item 99 of candidates in Group 2 or the high-score group were equal to or higher than 11. The 119 candidates were classified into this group. Then, the relevance between their scores on Item 99 and their questionnaire options is reported. Figure 9.12 indicates that no linear relation between those candidates' scores on Item 99 and their questionnaire options exists. The results of the Pearson correlation analysis shown in Table 9.28 also suggest that there is no significant correlation, because the value of *p* is $0.089 > 0.05$.

Then, according to their questionnaire options, 196 candidates were distributed into two groups for a second time: Group 1 and Group 2. Members in Group 1 didn't think they could reach the requirements of the *Standards*

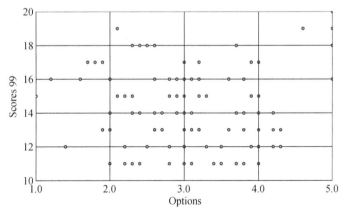

Figure 9.12 Scatter Diagram of Scores on Item 99 and Questionnaire Options (*n*=119)

Table 9.28   Correlations between Scores on Item 99 and Questionnaire Options ($n=119$)

		Scores on Item 99	Questionnaire options
Scores on Item 99	Pearson Correlation	1	0.157
	Sig. (2-tailed)		0.089
	n	119	119
Questionnaire options	Pearson Correlation	0.157	1
	Sig. (2-tailed)	0.089	
	n	119	119

Level 5. The mean of their questionnaire options was below or equal to 3. Examinees classified in Group 2 thought they could reach the requirements of the *Standards* Level 5. The mean of their questionnaire options was above 3.

97 candidates belonged Group 1. According to Figure 9.13, there exists no linear relation. Results of the Pearson correlation analysis are presented in Table 9.29, and the value of p is 0.468, which also shows no significant relevance.

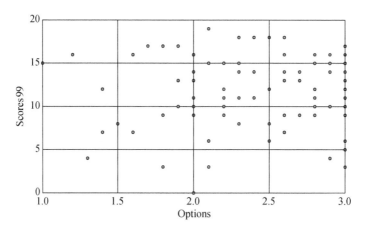

Figure 9.13   Scatter Diagram of Scores on Item 99 and Questionnaire Options ($n=97$)

Table 9.29 Correlations between Scores on Item 99 and Questionnaire Options ($n=97$)

		Scores on Item 99	Questionnaire options
Scores on Item 99	Pearson Correlation	1	0.075
	Sig. (2-tailed)		0.468
	n	97	97
Questionnaire options	Pearson Correlation	0.075	1
	Sig. (2-tailed)	0.468	
	n	97	97

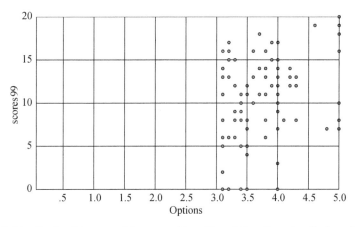

Figure 9.14 Scatter Diagram of Scores on Item 99 and Questionnaire Options ($n=99$)

In Group 2, there were 99 examinees. As observed in Figure 9.14, the scatter of their scores on Item 99 and their questionnaire options rises from the lower left corner to the top right-hand corner generally, which suggests that there seems to be a positive linear relation.

Then, a correlation analysis was adopted. According to Table 9.30, the value of p is $0.002 < 0.01$, which indicates that scores of candidates in Group 2 and their questionnaire options are significantly correlated at the level of 0.01. To have a further exploration, a regression analysis was then employed.

Table 9.30 Correlations between Scores on Item 99 and Questionnaire Options ($n=99$)

		Scores on Item 99	Questionnaire options
Scores on Item 99	Pearson Correlation	1	0.311**
	Sig. (2-tailed)		0.002
	n	99	99
Questionnaire options	Pearson Correlation	0.311**	1
	Sig. (2-tailed)	0.002	
	n	99	99

**. Correlation is significant at the 0.01 level (2-tailed).

First, to investigate whether candidates' self-evaluation data could predict their scores on Item 99, candidates' questionnaire options were regarded as the independent variable, and their scores on Item 99 as the dependent variable. As illustrated in Table 9.31, the coefficient of R Square is 0.097, which indicates the predictive power of the regression equation.

Table 9.31 Model Summary of Model 1

Model	R	R Square	Adjusted R Square	Std. Error of the Estimate
1	0.311[a]	0.097	0.084	4.687

Predictors: (Constant), options.

According to Table 9.32, the value of p equals 0.002 which is less than 0.01. Thus, there exists a significant linear relation between examinees' questionnaire options and their scores on Item 99.

Table 9.32 ANOVA Analysis of Model 1

Model		Sum of Squares	df	Mean Square	F	Sig.
1	Regression	227.683	1	227.683	10.364	0.002[b]
	Residual	2130.862	97	21.968		
	Total	2358.545	98			

Predictors: (Constant), options.

The value of p reported in Table 9.33 is 0.002. It indicates that the test of the coefficient is of statistical significance. In other words, candidates' questionnaire options can predict their scores on Item 99. The regression equation may be concluded as: $y = 1.067 + 2.666x$. In this equation, "x" refers to questionnaire options, and "y" refers to scores on Item 99.

Table 9.33　Coefficients of Model 1

Model		Unstandardized Coefficients		Standardized Coefficients	t	Sig.
		B	Std. Error	Beta		
1	(Constant)	1.067	3.186		0.335	0.738
	options	2.666	0.828	0.311	3.219	0.002

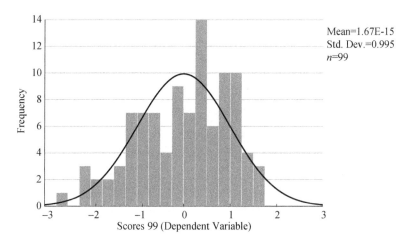

Figure 9.15　Histogram of Regression Standardized Residual in Model 1

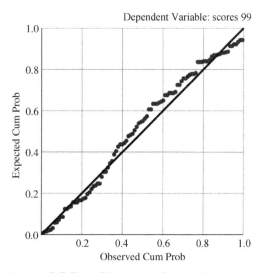

Figure 9.16　Normal P-P Plot of Regression Standardized Residual in Model 1

From Figure 9.15, it can be observed that the left side and right side are generally symmetric. As shown in Figure 9.16, points are roughly scattered on the oblique line. The normality of residual is not the most optimal, but it can be accepted. Thus, the regression equation of Model 1 passes the test of the normality of standardized residual.

Then, to investigate the predictive power of candidates' scores on the Item 99, the researcher regarded candidates' scores on Item 99 as the independent variable, and their questionnaire options as the dependent variable.

According to Table 9.34, the coefficient of R Square is 0.097, which suggests the predictive power of Model 2 (using candidates' scores on Item 99 to predict their questionnaire options).

As illustrated in the last column of Table 9.35, the value of p is 0.002. Therefore, there exists a significant linear relation between candidates' questionnaire options and their scores on Item 99. Besides, the regression model established or Model 2 is of statistical significance.

Table 9.34 Model Summary of Model 2

Model	R	R Square	Adjusted R Square	Std. Error of the Estimate
2	0.311[a]	0.097	0.087	0.5462

Predictors: (Constant), scores 99.

Table 9.35 ANOVA Analysis of Model 2

	Model	Sum of Squares	df	Mean Square	F	Sig.
2	Regression	3.092	1	3.092	10.364	0.002[b]
	Residual	28.936	97	0.298		
	Total	32.027	98			

Predictors: (Constant), scores 99.

Table 9.36 reports that the sig value is 0.002, which is less than 0.001. It suggests that the test of the coefficient is statistically significant. In other words, candidates' scores on Item 99 can predict their questionnaire options. And the regression equation may be expressed as: $y = 3.399 + 0.036x$ ("x" refers to candidates' scores on Item 99 and "y" refers to their questionnaire options).

Table 9.36 Coefficients of Model 2

Model		Unstandardized Coefficients		Standardized Coefficients	t	Sig.
		B	Std. Error	Beta		
2	(Constant)	3.399	0.138		24.716	0.000
	scores 99	0.036	0.011	0.311	3.219	0.002

From Figure 9.17, it shows that the left side and the right side are generally symmetric. Figure 9.18 indicates that points are roughly scattered on the oblique line. The normality of residual is not the most optimal, but it can be accepted. Therefore, the regression equation of Model 2 passes the test of the normality of standardized residual.

In summary, a significant positive linear relation can only be found between the questionnaire options of 99 examinees who think that they can reach the requirements of the *Standards* Level 5, and their scores on Item 99. In other words, those 99 examinees think that they can reach the requirements of the *Standards* Level 5, and their self-evaluation data is reliable.

According to those 99 candidates' self-evaluation, a group of borderline candidates were selected. The mean of their self-evaluation was the lowest among those 99 examinees. Table 9.37 presents the mean of questionnaire options and the scores on Item 99 of those borderline candidates.

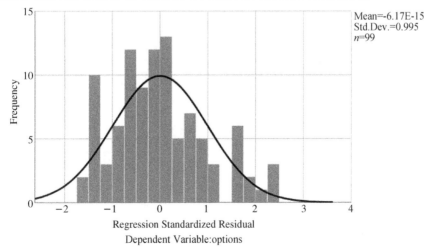

Figure 9.17 Histogram of Regression Standardized Residual in Model 2

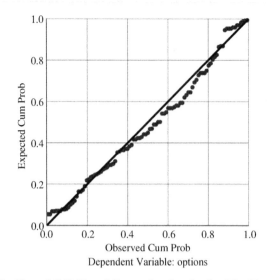

Figure 9.18 Normal P-P Plot of Regression Standardized Residual in Model 2

There are 12 borderline examinees. The average score of those 12 examinees is regarded as the cut-off score. Thus, the cut-off score is 9.9. Examinees whose scores on Item 99 are no less than 9.9 can be allocated to the *Standards* Level 5.

Table 9.37 A Description of Borderline Examinees

Examinee	The mean of their questionnaire options	Their scores on Item 99
1	3.1	13
2	3.1	14
3	3.1	16
4	3.1	0
5	3.1	5
6	3.1	14
7	3.1	16
8	3.1	6
9	3.1	14
10	3.1	11
11	3.1	2
12	3.1	8

9.3.4 The Relation between Examinees' Self-Evaluation and Their Scores on Item 100

A Pearson correlation analysis was adopted to explore the relation between candidates' scores on Item 100 and their questionnaire options. Before that a scatter diagram was drawn. According to the distribution of examinees' questionnaire data and their scores on Item 100 shown in Figure 9.19, no linear relation can be found. Then, the results of the Pearson correlation analysis reported in Table 9.38 further indicate that there is no significant correlation between candidates' scores on Item 100 and their questionnaire options, because the value of p is 0.226>0.05.

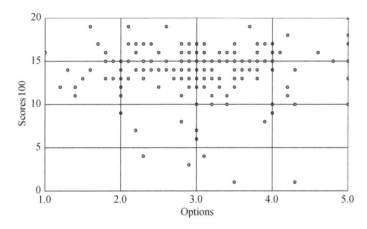

Figure 9.19 Scatter Diagram of Scores on Item 100 and Questionnaire Options ($n=196$)

Table 9.38 Correlations between Scores on Item 100 and Questionnaire Options ($n=196$)

		Scores on Item 100	Questionnaire options
Scores on Item 100	Pearson Correlation	1	0.087
	Sig. (2-tailed)		0.226
	n	196	196
Questionnaire options	Pearson Correlation	0.087	1
	Sig. (2-tailed)	0.226	
	n	196	196

To have a further exploration, based on their scores on Item 100, 196 examinees were divided into two groups: Group 1 and Group 2. Group 1 referred to the low-score group, while Group 2 stood for the high-score group.

In Group 1, there were 20 candidates. Their scores on Item 100 were lower than 11. First, as illustrated in Figure 9.20, no linear relation between candidates' scores on Item 100 and their questionnaire options can be found.

A correlation analysis was then employed. According to Table 9.39, there exists no significant correlation between those 20 candidates' scores on Item 100 and their questionnaire options, because the value of p is 0.464>0.05.

In Group 2 or the high-score group, there were 176 candidates, and their

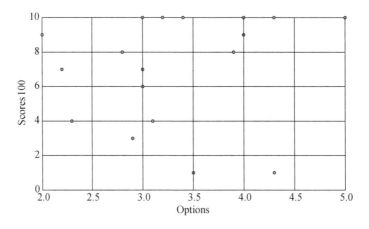

Figure 9.20 Scatter Diagram of Scores on Item 100 and Questionnaire Options ($n=20$)

Table 9.39 Correlations between Scores on Item 100 and Questionnaire Options ($n=20$)

		Scores on Item 100	Questionnaire options
	Pearson Correlation	1	0.174
Scores on Item 100	Sig. (2-tailed)		0.464
	n	20	20
	Pearson Correlation	0.174	1
Questionnaire options	Sig. (2-tailed)	0.464	
	n	20	20

scores on Item 100 were higher than or equal to 11. As demonstrated in Figure 9.21, the distribution of 176 candidates' scores on Item 100 and their questionnaire options increases from the lower left corner to the top right corner roughly, which means that there may exist a positive linear relation. After that, a Pearson correlation analysis was employed. According to Table 9.40, the value of p is 0.001<0.01. Therefore, the correlation is significant at the 0.01 level.

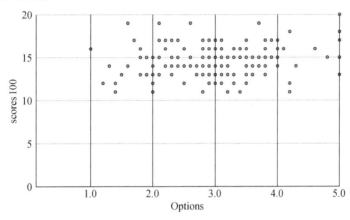

Figure 9.21 Scatter Diagram of Scores on Item 100 and Questionnaire Options ($n=176$)

Table 9.40 Correlations between Scores on Item 100 and Questionnaire Options ($n=176$)

		Scores on Item 100	Questionnaire options
Scores on Item 100	Pearson Correlation	1	0.251**
	Sig. (2-tailed)		0.001
	n	176	176
Questionnaire options	Pearson Correlation	0.251**	1
	Sig. (2-tailed)	0.001	
	n	176	176

** . Correlation is significant at the 0.01 level (2-tailed).

Since there existed a significant correlation, a regression analysis was then applied. First, 176 candidates' questionnaire options were set as the independent variable, and their scores on Item 100 as the dependent variable.

The coefficient of R Square is 0.063 according to the third column of Table 9.41.

As demonstrated in Table 9.42, the sig value is 0.001<0.01. It indicates a significant linear relation between candidates' questionnaire options and their scores on Item 100. Besides, the regression model or Model 1 is of statistical significance.

Table 9.41　Model Summary of Model 1

Model	R	R Square	Adjusted R Square	Std. Error of the Estimate
1	0.251[a]	0.063	0.057	1.741

Predictors: (Constant), scores.

Table 9.42　ANOVA Analysis of Model 1

Model		Sum of Squares	df	Mean Square	F	Sig.
1	Regression	35.375	1	35.375	11.672	0.001[b]
	Residual	527.353	174	3.031		
	Total	562.727	175			

Predictors: (Constant), options. Dependent Variable: scores 100.

Table 9.43　Coefficients of Model 1

Model		Unstandardized Coefficients		Standardized Coefficients	t	Sig.
		B	Std. Error	Beta		
1	(Constant)	13.064	0.479		27.301	0.000
	scores	0.507	0.148	0.251	3.416	0.001

According to the last column of Table 9.43, the value of p is 0.001, which suggests that the test of the coefficient is statistically significant. Thus, candidates' questionnaire options can predict their scores on Item 100, and the regression equation may be expressed as: $y = 13.064 + 0.507x$ ("x" refers to candidates' questionnaire options and "y" refers to their scores on Item 100).

According to Figure 9.22, it can be observed that the left and right sides are generally symmetric. As illustrated in Figure 9.23, points are roughly scattered on the oblique line. The normality of residual is not the most

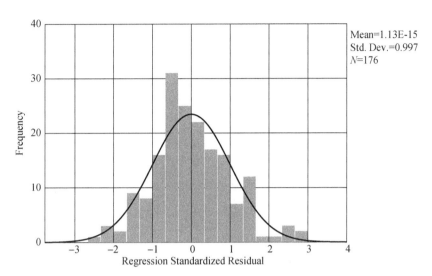

Figure 9.22　Histogram of Regression Standardized Residual in Model 1

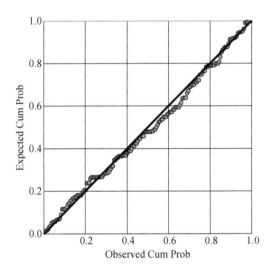

Figure 9.23　Normal P-P Plot of Regression Standardized Residual in Model 1

optimal, but it can be accepted. As a result, the regression equation of Model 1 passes the test of the normality of standardized residual.

To explore the predictive power of candidates' scores on Item 100, 176 candidates' scores on Item 100 were then set as the independent variable, and their questionnaire options as the dependent variable in the regression analysis. As shown in Table 9.44, the coefficient of R Square is 0.063, which is usually considered an important factor in analyzing the predictive power of a regression equation.

Table 9.44 Model Summary of Model 2

Model	R	R Square	Adjusted R Square	Std. Error of the Estimate
2	0.251[a]	0.063	0.057	0.8604

Predictors: (Constant), options.

According to Table 9.45, the value of p equals 0.001, which is less than 0.01. Therefore, the regression model or Model 2 is of statistical significance.

Table 9.45 ANOVA Analysis of Model 2

Model		Sum of Squares	df	Mean Square	F	Sig.
2	Regression	8.640	1	8.640	11.672	0.001[b]
	Residual	128.800	174	0.740		
	Total	137.440	175			

Predictors: (Constant), options.

As illustrated in Table 9.46, the value of p is 0.001, which means that the test of the coefficient is of statistical significance. Thus, candidates' scores on Item 100 have a predictive power (R Square=0.063) to their questionnaire options. The regression equation may be concluded as: $y=1.285+0.124x$ ("x" refers to candidates' scores on Item 100, and "y" refers to their questionnaire options).

Table 9.46 Coefficients of Model 2

Model		Unstandardized Coefficients		Standardized Coefficients	t	Sig.
		B	Std. Error	Beta		
2	(Constant)	1.285	0.535		2.403	0.017
	scores 100	0.124	0.036	0.251	3.416	0.001

From Figure 9.24, it can be observed that the left and right sides are generally symmetric. As shown in Figure 9.25, points are roughly scattered on the oblique line. The normality of residual is not the most optimal, but it can be accepted. Hence, the regression equation passes the test of the

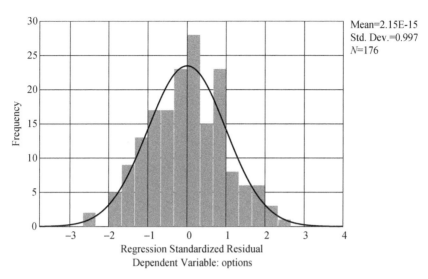

Figure 9.24 Histogram of Regression Standardized Residual in Model 2

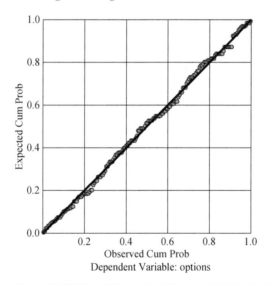

Figure 9.25 Normal P-P Plot of Regression Standardized Residual in Model 2

normality of standardized residual.

So far, the grouping is based on candidates' scores on Item 100. Then, according to their questionnaire options, 196 candidates were classified into two groups again: Group 1 and Group 2. Members of Group 1 didn't think they could reach the requirements of the *Standards* Level 5. The mean of their questionnaire options was less than or equalled 3. Examinees involved in

Group 2 thought they could reach the requirements of the *Standards* Level 5. The mean of their questionnaire options was higher than 3.

Totally, 97 candidates belonged to Group 1. First, a scatter diagram was drawn to explore the relation between 97 candidates' scores on Item 100 and their questionnaire options. According to Figure 9.26, no linear relation can be found.

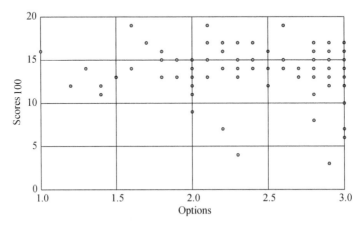

Figure 9.26 Scatter Diagram of Scores on Item 100 and Questionnaire Options ($n=97$)

Then, according to the results of the Pearson correlation analysis illustrated in Table 9.47, the value of p is 0.510, which indicates that there exists no significant correlation between those candidates' scores on Item 100 and their questionnaire options.

Table 9.47 Correlations between Scores on Item 100 and Questionnaire Options ($n=97$)

		Scores on Item 100	Questionnaire options
Scores on Item 100	Pearson Correlation	1	−0.068
	Sig. (2-tailed)		0.510
	n	97	97
Questionnaire options	Pearson Correlation	−0.068	1
	Sig. (2-tailed)	0.510	
	n	97	97

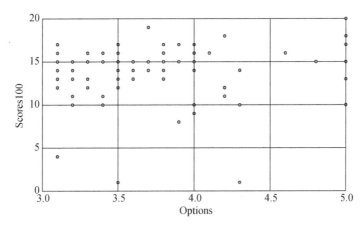

Figure 9.27   Scatter Diagram of Scores on Item 100 and Questionnaire Options ($n=99$)

In Group 2, there were 99 candidates. As observed in Figure 9.27, there exists no linear relation between those candidates' questionnaire options and their scores on Item 100. Then, a correlation analysis was adopted. According to Table 9.48, the value of p is $0.109 > 0.05$. It reflects that there is no significant correlation between those candidates' scores on Item 100 and their questionnaire options.

Table 9.48   Correlations between Scores on Item 100 and Questionnaire Options ($n=99$)

		Scores on Item 100	Questionnaire options
Scores on Item 100	Pearson Correlation	1	0.162
	Sig. (2-tailed)		0.109
	n	99	99
Questionnaire options	Pearson Correlation	0.162	1
	Sig. (2-tailed)	0.109	
	n	99	99

*. Correlation is significant at the 0.05 level (2-tailed).

To sum up, a significant positive linear relation can only be identified between the questionnaire options of 176 examinees who get a high score on Item 100, and their scores on Item 100. In other words, those 176 examinees' self-evaluation data is relatively reliable.

Among those 176 candidates, a group of borderline candidates were selected according to their self-evaluation data, and the mean of their self-evaluation was the lowest among those 176 examinees. Totally, there are 11 borderline candidates. Table 9.49 presents their self-evaluation data and their scores on Item 100. Their average scores on Item 100 can be regarded as the cut-off score. Therefore, the cut-off score is 14.7. It means that examinees whose scores on Item 100 are higher than or equal to 14.7 can be allocated to the *Standards* Level 5.

Table 9.49 A Description of Borderline Examinees

Examinee	The mean of their questionnaire options	Their scores on Item 100
1	3.1	14
2	3.1	17
3	3.1	12
4	3.1	13
5	3.1	13
6	3.1	14
7	3.1	15
8	3.1	15
9	3.1	16
10	3.1	16
11	3.1	17

9.3.5 Summary

According to examinees' self-evaluation questionnaire data, examinees thought that they could reach the requirements of the *Standards* Level 5. Since performance standards should be set on the basis of reliable examinees' self-evaluation, the correlation between examinees' questionnaire options and their HSK scores was analyzed.

The results of the correlation analysis showed that a significant positive linear relation could be found between the questionnaire options of 99 examinees who thought they could reach the requirements of the *Standards* Level 5, and their overall scores of Items 99 and 100, as well as between those examinees' questionnaire options and their scores on Item 99. Besides, a significant positive linear relation could also be identified between the questionnaire options of 176 examinees who got a high score on Item 100, and their scores on Item 100. In other words, the self-evaluation data of those two groups of examinees were relatively reliable. However, the correlations were at a low level.

Based on reliable self-evaluation data, the performance standards were set. Examinees whose overall scores on Items 99 and 100 were no less than 23.75, scores on Item 99 were at least 9.9, or scores on Item 100 were no less than 14.7 could be allocated to the *Standards* Level 5.

9.4 Results for Research Question Four

According to the results of Research Question 3, the cut-off scores or performance standards were set based on HSK Level 5 test takers' self-evaluation. Research Question 4 aims at addressing the actual performance of HSK Level 5 test takers in relation to the *Standards* through quantitative and qualitative methods, and then setting the performance standards. 30 examinees' scripts of Item 99 and their scripts of Item 100 were selected by the Center for Language Education and Cooperation. Their scores on Item 99 and Item 100 were provided as well.

Totally, the 30 scripts of Item 99 (Scripts 1 – 30) were chosen for the present study. Scripts 1 – 2, 7 – 8, 13 – 14, 19 – 20 and 25 – 26 of Item 99 were selected from the low-score group. Scripts 3 – 4, 9 – 10, 15 – 16, 21 – 22 and 27 – 28 of Item 99 belonged to the intermediate group. Scripts 5 – 6, 11 – 12, 17 – 18, 23 – 24 and 29 – 30 were chosen from the high-score group.

30 scripts of Item 100 (Script 31 – 60) were also provided. Scripts 31 – 32, 37 – 38, 43 – 44, 49 – 50 and 55 – 56 of Item 100 were selected from the low score group. Scripts 33 – 34, 39 – 40, 45 – 46, 51 – 52 and 57 – 58 of Item 100

belonged to the intermediate group. Scripts 35 – 36, 41 – 42, 47 – 48, 53 – 54 and 59 – 60 were chosen from the high-score group.

As a quantitative method, 10 questionnaires (Questionnaires 2 to 11) were designed. Each of those 10 questionnaires provided 6 different scripts of Item 99 or Item 100. Among those 6 scripts, 2 belonged to the low-score group, 2 in the intermediate group, and another 2 were chosen from the high-score group. In each questionnaire, there were 36 items in the form of Likert 5-point scales.

Among the 55 experts who had answered the questionnaire for making a content alignment, only 30 of them judged the relation between examinees' written scripts and the *Standards*. Those 30 experts were equally divided into two groups, i.e. Group 1 and Group 2. Each member of Group 1 evaluated 6 scripts of Item 99, while each expert in Group 2 judged 6 scripts of Item 100. To ensure validity, each script should be evaluated by 3 experts. Thus, experts in Group 1 and Group 2 were further divided into 5 teams. In each team, there were 3 experts, and they judged the same 6 scripts. In other words, the 3 experts in the same team answered the same questionnaire. There were 10 teams of experts, which explained the reason why 10 questionnaires were designed.

As a qualitative method, 4 experts were invited to have an interview based on their answers to the questionnaire items. The 4 experts (Interviewees A, B, C and D) also attended the interview designed for Research Question 2.

9.4.1 Results of the Quantitative Analysis

In terms of the alignment between the 30 candidates' scripts of Item 99 (Scripts 1 – 30) and the *Standards*, the results of the descriptive analysis are shown in Table 9.50. Each script was aligned with 6 descriptors by 3 experts. Thus, the value of n equals 18.

The standard deviations are around 1. Levels of skewness and kurtosis mostly range from -2 to 2. Those results indicate a stable and basically reasonable distribution of the questionnaire data.

The minimum of the questionnaire data is in the range of 1 to 3. The maximum of the questionnaire data is in the range of 2 to 5. Besides, the mean of the questionnaire data is mostly around 3, which suggests that the actual performance of HSK Level 5 test takers can basically reflect the requirements of the *Standards* Level 5.

Table 9.50　Descriptive Statistics of Experts' Judgment on Scripts of Item 99 ($n=18$)

Script	Minimum	Maximum	Mean	Std. Deviation	Skewness		Kurtosis	
	Statistic	Statistic	Statistic	Statistic	Statistic	Std. Error	Statistic	Std. Error
1	1.00	4.00	2.833 3	0.923 55	−0.140	0.536	−0.910	1.038
2	1.00	2.00	1.388 9	0.501 63	0.498	0.536	−1.987	1.038
3	2.00	5.00	2.777 8	1.003 26	0.892	0.536	−0.553	1.038
4	1.00	4.00	2.444 4	0.704 79	0.219	0.536	0.201	1.038
5	1.00	4.00	2.722 2	1.017 82	−0.498	0.536	−0.651	1.038
6	2.00	5.00	3.333 3	1.028 99	−0.405	0.536	−1.469	1.038
7	2.00	4.00	3.388 9	0.697 80	−0.724	0.536	−0.481	1.038
8	2.00	4.00	3.111 1	0.676 40	−0.132	0.536	−0.531	1.038
9	2.00	4.00	3.166 7	0.785 91	−0.318	0.536	−1.241	1.038
10	3.00	4.00	3.222 2	0.427 79	1.461	0.536	0.137	1.038
11	3.00	4.00	3.777 8	0.427 79	−1.461	0.536	0.137	1.038
12	2.00	5.00	3.555 6	0.855 59	0.441	0.536	−0.489	1.038
13	1.00	4.00	1.944 4	0.937 60	1.083	0.536	0.913	1.038
14	1.00	4.00	1.333 3	0.840 17	2.604	0.536	6.257	1.038
15	1.00	4.00	3.055 6	0.937 60	−0.602	0.536	−0.533	1.038
16	1.00	5.00	2.888 9	1.231 40	0.022	0.536	−1.412	1.038
17	3.00	5.00	4.388 9	0.697 80	−0.724	0.536	−0.481	1.038
18	3.00	5.00	4.388 9	0.607 68	−0.408	0.536	−0.513	1.038
19	1.00	3.00	1.555 6	0.615 70	0.616	0.536	−0.391	1.038
20	1.00	4.00	2.500 0	0.923 55	0.252	0.536	−0.602	1.038
21	2.00	4.00	3.222 2	0.646 76	−0.230	0.536	−0.411	1.038

continued

Script	Minimum	Maximum	Mean	Std. Deviation	Skewness		Kurtosis	
	Statistic	Statistic	Statistic	Statistic	Statistic	Std. Error	Statistic	Std. Error
22	2.00	4.00	3.222 2	0.548 32	0.159	0.536	0.181	1.038
23	2.00	5.00	3.555 6	0.855 59	0.441	0.536	−0.489	1.038
24	2.00	5.00	3.944 4	1.055 64	−0.554	0.536	−0.881	1.038
25	1.00	4.00	1.888 9	1.022 62	0.616	0.536	−1.075	1.038
26	1.00	2.00	1.055 6	0.235 70	4.243	0.536	18.000	1.038
27	1.00	3.00	1.888 9	0.471 40	−0.452	0.536	2.157	1.038
28	1.00	3.00	1.944 4	0.539 30	−0.073	0.536	1.213	1.038
29	3.00	4.00	3.555 6	0.511 31	−0.244	0.536	−2.199	1.038
30	2.00	4.00	3.277 8	0.574 51	−0.022	0.536	−0.255	1.038

To investigate the reliability of experts' judgment, the researcher made a correlation analysis between experts' judgment on scripts and the actual scores of those scripts. First, a scatter diagram was drawn. As observed in Figure 9.28, there is probably a positive linear relation.

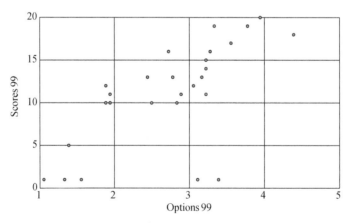

Figure 9.28 Scatter Diagram of Experts' Judgment and Scores of Scripts of Item 99 ($n=30$)

Then, a Pearson correlation analysis was employed. As observed in Table 9.51, there is a possible significant relation at the 0.01 level. Therefore, experts' judgment on the scripts of Item 99 is relatively reliable.

Table 9.51 Correlations between Experts' Judgment and Scores of Scripts of Item 99 ($n=30$)

		Experts' judgment	Scores of scripts of Item 99
Experts' judgment	Pearson Correlation	1	0.704**
	Sig. (2-tailed)		0.000
	n	30	30
Scores of scripts of Item 99	Pearson Correlation	0.704**	1
	Sig. (2-tailed)	0.000	
	n	30	30

**. Correlation is significant at the 0.01 level (2-tailed).

To have a further exploration, a regression analysis was adopted. Experts' judgment or the questionnaire option was set as the independent variable first. Table 9.52 presents that the coefficient of R Square is 0.495.

Table 9.52 Model Summary of Model 1

Model	R	R Square	Adjusted R Square	Std. Error of the Estimate
1	0.704[a]	0.495	0.477	4.306

Predictors: (Constant), options99.

Table 9.53 ANOVA Analysis of Model 1

Model		Sum of Squares	df	Mean Square	F	Sig.
1	Regression	508.816	1	508.816	27.448	0.000[b]
	Residual	519.051	28	18.538		
	Total	1027.867	29			

Predictors: (Constant), options99.

In Table 9.53, the sig value is lower than 0.001, so the regression model is significant statistically. According to Table 9.54, the test of the coefficient is of statistical significance, because the value of $p<0.001$. Hence, experts' judgment on scripts can be used to predict the actual scores of those scripts. The regression equation may be expressed as: $y=4.729x-1.719$ ("x" refers to experts' judgment or their questionnaire options, and "y" refers to the actual scores of scripts).

Table 9.54   Coefficients of Model 1

Model		Unstandardized Coefficients		Standardized Coefficients	t	Sig.
		B	Std. Error	Beta		
1	(Constant)	−1.719	2.685		−0.640	0.527
	options99	4.729	0.903	0.704	5.239	0.000

Figure 9.29 shows that the left and right sides are generally symmetric. As presented in Figure 9.30, points are roughly scattered on the oblique line. The normality of residual is not the most optimal, but it can be accepted. Hence, the regression equation passes the test of the normality of standardized residual.

Then, the actual scores of the scripts should be set as the independent variable, experts' judgement as the dependent variable for a regression analysis. From the Table 9.55, the coefficient of R Square is 0.495 which indicates the predictive power of Model 2 (using the actual scores of scripts to predict experts' judgment). The regression model or Model 2 is significant, as the value of p shown in Table 9.56 is lower than 0.001. According to Table 9.57, the value of p is lower than 0.001. Hence, the test of the coefficient is largely significant.

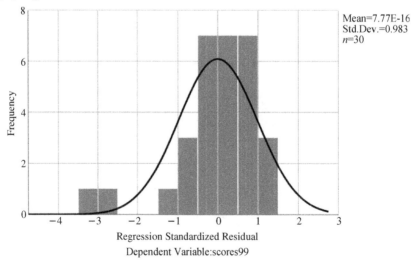

Figure 9.29   Histogram of Regression Standardized Residual in Model 1

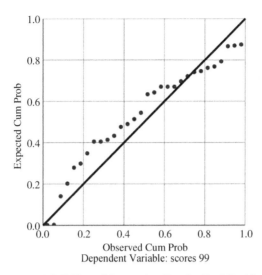

Figure 9.30　Normal P-P Plot of Regression Standardized Residual in Model 1

Table 9.55　Model Summary of Model 2

Model	R	R Square	Adjusted R Square	Std. Error of the Estimate
1	0.704[a]	0.495	0.477	0.640 536 0

Predictors: (Constant), scores 99.

Table 9.56　ANOVA Analysis of Model 2

Model		Sum of Squares	df	Mean Square	F	Sig.
1	Regression	11.262	1	11.262	27.448	0.000[b]
	Residual	11.488	28	0.410		
	Total	22.750	29			

Predictors: (Constant), scores 99.

Table 9.57　Coefficients of Model 2

Model		Unstandardized Coefficients		Standardized Coefficients	t	Sig.
		B	Std. Error	Beta		
1	(Constant)	1.616	0.262		6.170	0.000
	Scores 99	0.105	0.020	0.704	5.239	0.000

To sum up, the actual scores have the predictive power to experts' judgment, and the regression equation may be concluded as: $y = 0.105x +$

1.616 ("x" stands for the actual scores of the scripts, and "y" represents experts' judgment). Figure 9.31 and Figure 9.32 show that the normality of residual is not the most optimal, but it can be accepted. Thus, the regression equation passes the test of the normality of standardized residual.

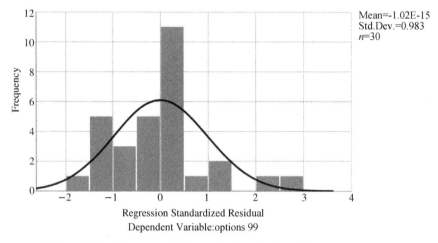

Figure 9.31   Histogram of Regression Standardized Residual in Model 2

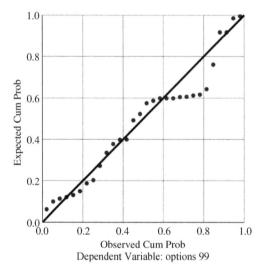

Figure 9.32   Normal P-P Plot of Regression Standardized Residual in Model 2

In conclusion, experts' judgment on the scripts of Item 99 is reliable. There is a significant positive linear relation between experts' judgment on the scripts of Item 99 and the actual scores of the scripts. Based on experts' judgment, a cut-off score will be provided to allocate examinees of HSK Level 5 into two proficiency levels: Level 5 or Level 5 minus.

Totally, 16 scripts of Item 99 can reflect the requirements of the *Standards* Level 5. According to the descriptive statistics shown in Table 9.50, the mean of experts' judgment on those 16 scripts is above 3. The borderline performance is reflected by Script 15, as the mean of experts' judgment on it is the smallest among the 16 scripts. The score of Script 15 can be considered as the cut-off score which is 12. It means that examinees whose scores on Item 99 are higher than or equal to 12 can be allocated to the *Standards* Level 5.

To explore the relation between the scripts of Item 99 and each of the six descriptors, a one-way ANOVA analysis was employed. According to Table 9.58, the value of p is $0.017 < 0.05$. It indicates that a significant difference exists. To have a further exploration, a post-hoc test was then applied.

Table 9.58 Differences among Experts' Judgment on Each Descriptor

	Sum of Squares	df	Mean Square	F	Sig.
Between Groups	18.289	5	3.658	2.788	0.017
Within Groups	700.644	534	1.312		
Total	718.933	539			

As illustrated in Table 9.59, experts' judgement on Descriptor 4 significantly differs from their judgment on Descriptors 1 and 3 respectively at the 0.05 level, as the value of p is lower than 0.05. Similarly, a significant difference between the judgment on Descriptor 6 and Descriptor 1 exists. Because the value of p is $0.023 < 0.05$.

Furthermore, according to the third column of Table 9.59, the degree of the alignment between scripts and Descriptor 4 is lower than that between scripts and Descriptor 1, as well as that between scripts and Descriptor 3. Similarly, the degree of the alignment between scripts and Descriptor 6 is lower than that between scripts and Descriptor 1.

As for the alignment between the scripts of Item 100 (Scripts 31-60) and the *Standards*, the results of the descriptive analysis are shown in Table 9.60. The minimum of experts' judgment on most scripts is 1 or 2, and the maximum of experts' judgment on most scripts is 4 or 5. The mean of experts' judgment on most scripts is above 2. The standard deviations, and levels of skewness and kurtosis reflect the stable and reasonable distribution of the questionnaire data.

Table 9.59 Multiple Comparisons between the Alignment on Each Descriptor

(I) Descriptor	(J) Descriptor	Mean Difference (I-J)	Std. Error	Sig.	95% Confidence Interval	
					Lower Bound	Upper Bound
1	2	0.255 56	0.170 75	0.135	−0.079 9	0.591 0
	3	0.088 89	0.170 75	0.603	−0.246 5	0.424 3
	4	0.555 56*	0.170 75	0.001	0.220 1	0.891 0
	5	0.311 11	0.170 75	0.069	−0.024 3	0.646 5
	6	0.388 89*	0.170 75	0.023	0.053 5	0.724 3
2	1	−0.255 56	0.170 75	0.135	−0.591 0	0.079 9
	3	−0.166 67	0.170 75	0.329	−0.502 1	0.168 8
	4	0.300 00	0.170 75	0.080	−0.035 4	0.635 4
	5	0.055 56	0.170 75	0.745	−0.279 9	0.391 0
	6	0.133 33	0.170 75	0.435	−0.202 1	0.468 8
3	1	−0.088 89	0.170 75	0.603	−0.424 3	0.246 5
	2	0.166 67	0.170 75	0.329	−0.168 8	0.502 1
	4	0.466 67*	0.170 75	0.006	0.131 2	0.802 1
	5	0.222 22	0.170 75	0.194	−0.113 2	0.557 7
	6	0.300 00	0.170 75	0.080	−0.035 4	0.635 4

continued

(I) Descriptor	(J) Descriptor	Mean Difference (I-J)	Std. Error	Sig.	95% Confidence Interval	
					Lower Bound	Upper Bound
4	1	−0.555 56*	0.170 75	0.001	−0.891 0	−0.220 1
	2	−0.300 00	0.170 75	0.080	−0.635 4	0.035 4
	3	−0.466 67*	0.170 75	0.006	−0.802 1	−0.131 2
	5	−0.244 44	0.170 75	0.153	−0.579 9	0.091 0
	6	−0.166 67	0.170 75	0.329	−0.502 1	0.168 8
5	1	−0.311 11	0.170 75	0.069	−0.646 5	0.024 3
	2	−0.055 56	0.170 75	0.745	−0.391 0	0.279 9
	3	−0.222 22	0.170 75	0.194	−0.557 7	0.113 2
	4	0.244 44	0.170 75	0.153	−0.091 0	0.579 9
	6	0.077 78	0.170 75	0.649	−0.257 7	0.413 2
6	1	−0.388 89*	0.170 75	0.023	−0.724 3	−0.053 5
	2	−0.133 33	0.170 75	0.435	−0.468 8	0.202 1
	3	−0.300 00	0.170 75	0.080	−0.635 4	0.035 4
	4	0.166 67	0.170 75	0.329	−0.168 8	0.502 1
	5	−0.077 78	0.170 75	0.649	−0.413 2	0.257 7

*. The mean difference is significant at the 0.05 level.

To investigate the reliability of experts' judgment, the researcher made a correlation analysis between experts' judgment on the scripts of Item 100 and the actual scores of those scripts. First of all, a scatter diagram was made. It can be observed in Figure 9.33 that there is probably a positive linear relation.

Table 9.60　Descriptive Statistics of Experts' Judgment on Scripts of Item 100 ($n=30$)

Script	Minimum	Maximum	Mean	Std. Deviation	Skewness		Kurtosis	
	Statistic	Statistic	Statistic	Statistic	Statistic	Std. Error	Statistic	Std. Error
31	1	4	2.72	0.752	−0.406	0.536	0.465	1.038
32	1	4	2.61	0.698	−0.445	0.536	0.462	1.038
33	1	5	2.89	1.023	0.244	0.536	−0.360	1.038

continued

Script	Minimum	Maximum	Mean	Std. Deviation	Skewness		Kurtosis	
	Statistic	Statistic	Statistic	Statistic	Statistic	Std. Error	Statistic	Std. Error
34	2	5	3.33	0.686	0.683	0.536	0.930	1.038
35	1	4	3.33	0.767	−1.565	0.536	3.978	1.038
36	2	5	3.50	0.707	0.000	0.536	0.118	1.038
37	2	4	2.94	0.873	0.116	0.536	−1.730	1.038
38	1	3	2.00	0.343	0.000	0.536	8.500	1.038
39	2	4	2.39	0.698	1.613	0.536	1.405	1.038
40	2	4	2.72	0.752	0.529	0.536	−0.933	1.038
41	2	4	2.83	0.857	0.350	0.536	−1.578	1.038
42	2	4	2.61	0.778	0.852	0.536	−0.706	1.038
43	1	4	2.17	0.707	0.873	0.536	1.906	1.038
44	1	3	1.67	0.686	0.547	0.536	−0.584	1.038
45	2	5	3.33	0.767	1.076	0.536	1.071	1.038
46	2	4	2.89	0.832	0.224	0.536	−1.518	1.038
47	3	4	3.44	0.511	0.244	0.536	−2.199	1.038
48	4	5	4.22	0.428	1.461	0.536	0.137	1.038
49	1	4	2.44	0.784	0.618	0.536	0.147	1.038
50	1	4	1.39	0.979	2.469	0.536	4.931	1.038
51	1	4	2.17	0.924	0.140	0.536	−0.910	1.038
52	1	4	2.67	0.907	0.236	0.536	−0.893	1.038
53	1	4	2.67	0.840	0.074	0.536	−0.472	1.038
54	1	4	2.67	0.907	0.236	0.536	−0.893	1.038
55	2	4	2.89	0.758	0.195	0.536	−1.118	1.038
56	2	3	2.44	0.511	0.244	0.536	−2.199	1.038
57	2	4	3.56	0.705	−1.354	0.536	0.654	1.038
58	2	4	2.89	0.583	−0.016	0.536	0.413	1.038
59	2	4	3.83	0.514	−3.239	0.536	10.494	1.038
60	2	5	3.83	0.786	−0.500	0.536	0.517	1.038

Considering the results of the Pearson correlation analysis shown in Table 9.61, the relation between experts' judgment on the scripts of Item 100 and the actual scores of those scripts is significant at the 0.01 level. To have a deeper grasp of the relation, a regression analysis was then adopted.

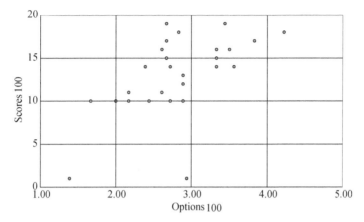

Figure 9.33 Scatter Diagram of Experts' Judgment and Scores of Scripts of Item 100 ($n=30$)

Table 9.61 Correlations between Experts' Judgment and Scores of Scripts of Item 100 ($n=30$)

		Scores of scripts of Item 100	Experts' judgment
Scores of scripts of Item 100	Pearson Correlation	1	0.602**
	Sig. (2-tailed)		0.000
	n	30	30
Experts' judgment	Pearson Correlation	0.602**	1
	Sig. (2-tailed)	0.000	
	n	30	30

**. Correlation is significant at the 0.01 level (2-tailed).

In order to analyze whether experts' judgment on scripts can predict the actual scores of those scripts, the researcher took experts' judgment as the independent variable, and actual scores as the dependent variable first.

The coefficient of R Square presented in Table 9.62 is 0.363. Table 9.63 shows that the sig value is lower than 0.01. Given the results shown in Table 9.64, the test of the coefficient is significant statistically, and the regression

149

equation may be concluded as: $y=4.197x+1.103$ ("x" stands for experts' judgment or their questionnaire options, and "y" refers to the actual scores of scripts of Item 100). As indicated in Figure 9.34 and Figure 9.35, the normality of residual is not the most optimal, but it can be accepted. Thus, the regression equation passes the test of the normality of standardized residual.

Table 9.62　Model Summary of Model 1

Model	R	R Square	Adjusted R Square	Std. Error of the Estimate
1	0.602[a]	0.363	0.340	3.602

Predictors: (Constant), options 100.

Table 9.63　ANOVA Analysis of Model 1

Model		Sum of Squares	df	Mean Square	F	Sig.
1	Regression	206.748	1	206.748	15.936	0.000[b]
	Residual	363.252	28	12.973		
	Total	570.000	29			

Predictors: (Constant), options 100.

Table 9.64　Coefficients of Model 1

Model		Unstandardized Coefficients		Standardized Coefficients	t	Sig.
		B	Std. Error	Beta		
1	(Constant)	1.103	3.052		0.361	0.721
	options100	4.197	1.051	0.602	3.992	0.000

Then, the actual scores of the scripts of Item 100 were set as the independent variable to explore whether those scores could also predict experts' judgment. In Table 9.65, the coefficient of R Square is 0.363 which suggests the predictive power of Model 2 (using the actual scores to predict experts' judgment). The value of p or Sig. illustrated in Table 9.66 is lower than 0.001, so Model 2 is statistically significant.

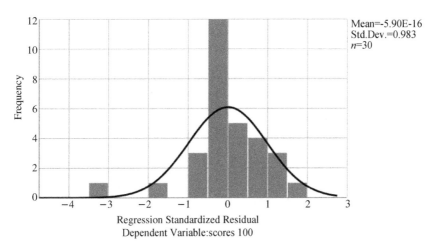

Figure 9.34 Histogram of Regression Standardized Residual in Model 1

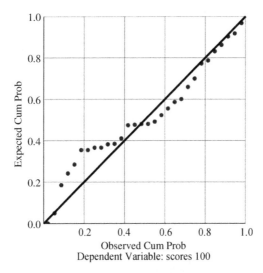

Figure 9.35 Normal P‑P Plot of Regression Standardized Residual in Model 1

Table 9.65 Model Summary of Model 2

Model	R	R Square	Adjusted R Square	Std. Error of the Estimate
1	0.602[a]	0.363	0.340	0.51685

a. Predictors: (Constant), scores100.

Table 9.66   ANOVA Analysis of Model 2

	Model	Sum of Squares	df	Mean Square	F	Sig.
1	Regression	4.257	1	4.257	15.936	0.000[b]
	Residual	7.480	28	0.267		
	Total	11.737	29			

Predictors: (Constant), scores 100.

Based on the results shown in Table 9.67, the test of the coefficient is significant, and the regression equation may be expressed as: $y = 0.086x + 1.711$ ("x" refers to the actual scores of the scripts of Item 100, and "y" stands for experts' judgment on their questionnaire options).

Table 9.67   Coefficients of Model 2

	Model	Unstandardized Coefficients		Standardized Coefficients	t	Sig.
		B	Std. Error	Beta		
1	(Constant)	1.711	0.297		5.765	0.000
	scores100	0.086	0.022	0.602	3.992	0.000

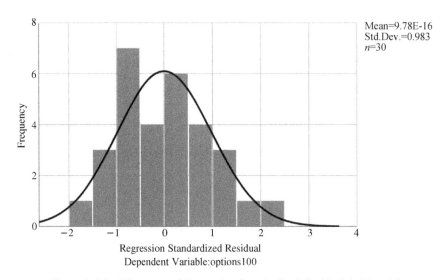

Figure 9.36   Histogram of Regression Standardized Residual in Model 2

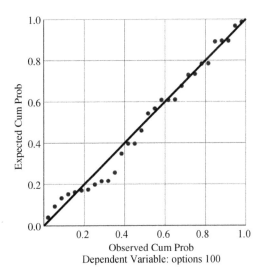

Figure 9.37 Normal P-P Plot of Regression Standardized Residual in Model 2

As observed in Figure 9.36, the left and right sides are generally symmetric. According to Figure 9.37, points are roughly scattered on the oblique line. The normality of residual is not the most optimal, but it can be accepted. Hence, the regression equation passes the test of the normality of standardized residual.

In conclusion, experts' judgment on the scripts of Item 100 is reliable, and there is a significant positive linear relation between experts' judgment on the scripts of Item 100 and the actual scores of those scripts. Based on experts' judgment, a cut-off score will be provided to allocate examinees of HSK Level 5 into two proficiency levels: Level 5 or Level 5 minus.

Totally, 9 scripts of Item 100 can reflect the requirements of the *Standards* Level 5. According to the descriptive statistics shown in Table 9.60, the mean of experts' judgment on those 9 scripts is higher than 3. The borderline performance is reflected by Scripts 34, 35 and 45, because the mean of experts' judgement on those 3 scripts is the smallest among the 9 scripts. Table 9.68 provides a description of the 3 scripts.

The average score of those 3 scripts can be considered as the cut-off score. Hence, the cut-off score is 15. In other words, examinees whose scores on the Item 100 are no less than 15 can be allocated to the *Standards* Level 5.

Table 9.68　A Description of Scripts 34, 35 and 45

Script	Experts' judgment	Actual scores
34	3.33	15
35	3.33	16
45	3.33	14

A one-way ANOVA was then adopted to explore whether there was a significant difference among the judgment on each of the six descriptors. According to Table 9.69, the value of p is $0.006 < 0.01$. Therefore, a significant difference exists.

Table 9.69　Differences among Experts' Judgment on Each Descriptor

	Sum of Squares	df	Mean Square	F	Sig.
Between Groups	15.031	5	3.006	3.308	0.006
Within Groups	485.300	534	0.909		
Total	500.331	539			

To further unveil the relation among the judgment on each descriptor, multiple comparisons were made. The independent variable was different descriptors and the dependent variable was questionnaire options.

From the results reported in Table 9.70, experts' judgment on Descriptor 4 is significantly different from their judgment on the other five descriptors at the 0.05 level respectively. Because the corresponding values of p are lower than 0.05. Moreover, according to the value of the mean difference, the degree of the alignment between the scripts of Item 100 and Descriptor 4 is the lowest or the most unsatisfactory.

▶▶▶ 第二部分：Aligning HSK Level 5 Writing Test with *Chinese Proficiency Grading Standards for International Chinese Language Education*

Table 9.70 Multiple Comparisons between the Alignment on Each Descriptor

(I) Descriptor	(J) Descriptor	Mean Difference (I-J)	Std. Error	Sig.	95% Confidence Interval	
					Lower Bound	Upper Bound
1	2	0.077 78	0.142 11	0.584	−0.201 4	0.356 9
	3	−0.055 56	0.142 11	0.696	−0.334 7	0.223 6
	4	0.455 56*	0.142 11	0.001	0.176 4	0.734 7
	5	0.033 33	0.142 11	0.815	−0.245 8	0.312 5
	6	0.144 44	0.142 11	0.310	−0.134 7	0.423 6
2	1	−0.077 78	0.142 11	0.584	−0.356 9	0.201 4
	3	−0.133 33	0.142 11	0.349	−0.412 5	0.145 8
	4	0.377 78*	0.142 11	0.008	0.098 6	0.656 9
	5	−0.044 44	0.142 11	0.755	−0.323 6	0.234 7
	6	0.066 67	0.142 11	0.639	−0.212 5	0.345 8
3	1	0.055 56	0.142 11	0.696	−0.223 6	0.334 7
	2	0.133 33	0.142 11	0.349	−0.145 8	0.412 5
	4	0.511 11*	0.142 11	0.000	0.231 9	0.790 3
	5	0.088 89	0.142 11	0.532	−0.190 3	0.368 1
	6	0.200 00	0.142 11	0.160	−0.079 2	0.479 2
4	1	−0.455 56*	0.142 11	0.001	−0.734 7	−0.176 4
	2	−0.377 78*	0.142 11	0.008	−0.656 9	−0.098 6
	3	−0.511 11*	0.142 11	0.000	−0.790 3	−0.231 9
	5	−0.422 22*	0.142 11	0.003	−0.701 4	−0.143 1
	6	−0.311 11*	0.142 11	0.029	−0.590 3	−0.031 9
5	1	−0.033 33	0.142 11	0.815	−0.312 5	0.245 8
	2	0.044 44	0.142 11	0.755	−0.234 7	0.323 6
	3	−0.088 89	0.142 11	0.532	−0.368 1	0.190 3
	4	0.422 22*	0.142 11	0.003	0.143 1	0.701 4
	6	0.111 11	0.142 11	0.435	−0.168 1	0.390 3

continued

(I) Descriptor	(J) Descriptor	Mean Difference (I-J)	Std. Error	Sig.	95% Confidence Interval	
					Lower Bound	Upper Bound
6	1	−0.144 44	0.142 11	0.310	−0.423 6	0.134 7
	2	−0.066 67	0.142 11	0.639	−0.345 8	0.212 5
	3	−0.200 00	0.142 11	0.160	−0.479 2	0.079 2
	4	0.311 11*	0.142 11	0.029	0.031 9	0.590 3
	5	−0.111 11	0.142 11	0.435	−0.390 3	0.168 1

*. The mean difference is significant at the 0.05 level.

9.4.2 Results of the Qualitative Analysis

In the interview, 2 experts (Interviewees A and B) made comments and gave a general description of the alignment between the scripts of Item 99 and the *Standards*. Meanwhile, another 2 experts (Interviewees C and D) accepted an interview about the alignment between the scripts of Item 100 and the *Standards*.

In terms of the alignment between the scripts of Item 99 and the *Standards*, both experts mentioned that the scripts could be hardly aligned with the *Standards* in terms of the requirements on the expected length and text genres. Instructions for Item 99 should be enriched in order to have a better degree of the alignment. Interviewees A and B made the judgment on Scripts 19 – 24 by answering the questionnaire. Parts of their replies are shown as follows:

Q. Do you think the scripts of Item 99 can be aligned with the *Standards* Level 5? And why?

Interviewee A: Generally speaking, those scripts can be aligned with Descriptors 1, 2, 3 and 5. Obviously, no script can meet the requirement of the expected length made by Descriptor 4. Descriptor 6 focuses on Chinese learners' ability to write expositions, but most candidates tend to write narratives instead of expositions according to the scripts shown in the questionnaire.

Although those candidates have the ability of write an article, their ability to write an article of a specific genre cannot be evaluated. It's urgent for us to release HSK Levels 7-9.

Interviewee B: Scripts can be hardly aligned with Descriptor 4 in terms of the expected length. Descriptor 4 requires learners to write an article of 450 Chinese characters. However, candidates only wrote an essay of 80 Chinese characters. It is necessary to set higher requirements on the expected length.

Interviewees C and D were invited to judge the relation between the scripts of Item 100 and the *Standards* Level 5. Both of them judged Scripts 49—54. They pointed out that the scripts could hardly be aligned with the *Standards* in terms of the requirements on the expected length and text genres. The Descriptors of the *Standards* should be precise and the instructions of Item 100 should be enriched. Parts of their replies are shown as follows:

Q. Do you think the scripts of Item 100 can be aligned with the *Standards* Level 5? And why?

Interviewee C: The degree of the alignment between the scripts and Descriptors 3, 4 and 5 is relatively better. Those six scripts provided in the questionnaire cannot reflect candidates' ability to write in different text genres and topics. The text genres and topics should be limited by the instructions of Item 100.

Interviewee D: Generally, I think the difficulty of Item 100 is actually lower than the requirements of the *Standards* Level 5. Descriptors require Chinese language learners to write expositions, argumentations and practical articles. That is to say, candidates should have the ability to write in various genres. But actually, candidates are good at writing narratives. All candidates wrote narratives, because Item 100 did not explicitly require them to write in a specific genre. In addition, in terms of the expected length, the *Standards* are more demanding as well. I think the requirements for candidates' scripts are not clearly described in the instructions. To have a better degree of the alignment between examinees' scripts and the *Standards*, appropriate rating criteria should be given in the instructions, such as smoothness in expression, informativeness in content and so on.

9.4.3 Summary

Since performance standards should be set on the basis of reliable experts' judgment, the correlation between experts' judgment and the actual scores of examinees' written scripts was analyzed.

The results of the correlation analysis showed that a significant positive linear relation could be identified between experts' judgment and the actual scores of examinees' written scripts, and the correlation was at a relatively satisfactory level. In other words, experts' judgment was reliable.

Based on reliable experts' judgment, the performance standards or cut-off scores were set. Examinees whose scores on Item 99 were at least 12, or scores on Item 100 were no less than 15 could be allocated to the *Standards* Level 5.

In addition, according to experts' judgment, Items 99 and 100 could be basically aligned with the *Standards* Level 5 from the perspective of examinees' actual performance. The degree of the alignment between Item 99 and each descriptor, as well as between Item 100 and each descriptor was significantly different. Specifically, the alignment between Item 99 and Descriptor 4, as well as between Item 100 and Descriptor 4 was relatively unsatisfactory.

10　Discussion

In this chapter, the results presented in Chapter Nine will be discussed from two aspects. Specifically, since this aligning study explores the content alignment and sets performance standards, discussions on the content alignment and performance standards will be carried out.

10.1　Discussion on the Content Alignment

In the process of aligning, the step of specification or content alignment aims at aligning tests with language proficiency standards from the content perspective, which contributes to increasing awareness that may help to improve the quality of tests (Figueras et al., 2005; Council of Europe, 2009). The preliminary alignment made in this step will be corroborated in the next aligning step which is usually called the standard setting. Only if the content of HSK can be matched with that of the *Standards* can the following steps of aligning be feasible. In the present study, the answers to Research Questions 1 and 2 are drawn from the content alignment.

The theoretical grounding of tests and language proficiency standards can reflect their constructs. Both the *Standards* and HSK are designed on the basis of the theory of communicative language ability, which indicates the possibility of the content alignment.

To have a more specific result of content alignment, both the qualitative evaluation made by two coders and the questionnaire answered by experts were adopted.

In terms of the qualitative evaluation, a content analysis of *HSK Rating Criteria*, *HSK Test Syllabus* and *HSK Test Item-writing Manual* is made from 4 aspects: the quantitative criteria, communicative functions, the communicative context and the quality of produced texts. *HSK Rating Criteria*, *HSK Test Syllabus* and *HSK Test Item-Writing Manual* can reflect the construct of HSK Level 5. The 4 dimensions of the content analysis are extracted according to the conceptual framework of the writing sub-scales of the *Standards* Level 5. The results of the qualitative evaluation show that HSK Level 5 writing test can possibly be aligned with the *Standards* Level 5.

As for the quantitative questionnaire survey, considering the focus of the present study, experts voluntarily participate in this study, and align Items 99 and 100 chosen from 3 sets of HSK Level 5 sample test papers with 6 selected descriptors in the writing sub-scales of the *Standards* Level 5. In addition to *HSK Rating Criteria*, *HSK Test Syllabus* and *HSK Test Item-Writing Manual*, the sample test paper can also manifest the construct of HSK Level 5.

Since the content alignment contributes to the improvement of the quality of the test concerned, a further discussion on experts' judgment will be beneficial to improve the quality of Item 99 and Item 100 in HSK Level 5 writing test.

A high-quality task should be constructed carefully, so as to allow candidates to perform to the best of their abilities, and to ensure that candidates' performance will not be affected by irrelevant variations. In this sense, clear instructions should be provided to candidates. Usually, the requirements of a writing task, including the expected genre, topic and length, are elicited by the instructions. Besides, the instruction of a writing task may also involve some stimulus materials, such as a passage, a picture and so on, which can inspire candidates to write (Weigle, 2002).

Therefore, when aligning Item 99 and Item 100 with the *Standards* from the content perspective, experts are likely to make their judgment based on the instructions, which is corroborated by interviewees' replies. As a result, the discussion on the content alignment should place emphasis on the analysis of the instructions in relation to the *Standards*. The contents of Item 99 and

Item 100 will be discussed respectively.

10.1.1 The Content of Item 99

The results of descriptive analysis and binomial test show that Item 99 can basically be aligned with the *Standards* from the content perspective, which further verifies the results of the qualitative content analysis of *HSK Rating Criteria*, *HSK Test Syllabus* and *HSK Test Item-Writing Manual*. But there still exists room for improvement. Specifically, according to the results of one-way ANOVA and post-hoc test, the content alignment between Item 99 and Descriptor 4 is relatively unsatisfactory, while a better content alignment between Item 99 and Descriptor 5 can be identified. To provide plausible explanations for those findings, it is necessary to have a closer look at the instructions of Item 99, as well as the statements of Descriptor 4 and Descriptor 5.

As the written instructions of Item 99 presented to candidates, the statement "please write a short article of about 80 Chinese characters by using all the words provided below" provides related information about the expected length of a produced text (Hanban, 2015: 1), and the stimulus material of Item 99 is several words.

Descriptor 5 stands for the statement "can complete writing tasks with comparatively appropriate vocabulary, basically correct sentence patterns, comparatively complete content, and comparatively clear expression" in the writing sub-scales of the *Standards* Level 5 (Center for Language Education and Cooperation, 2021b). It lays emphasis on the quality of written production or performance, especially the complexity, accuracy, and fluency of learners' written production or performance.

The satisfactory content alignment between Item 99 and Descriptor 5 found in the present study is consistent with the previous study. Interviewee A have mentioned that only basic requirements for learners' writing are covered by Descriptor 5. In other words, a writing task can always evaluate whether examinees can meet the requirements of Descriptor 5 or not, which suggests the possibility of relating Item 99 with Descriptor 5. In this sense, as the focuses of Descriptor 5, complexity, accuracy and fluency serve as basic indicators of rating learners' written production or performance and evaluating learners' language proficiency.

During the past decades, scholars have shown great interest in the quality of written production or performance. Generally, a high-rated written script tends to include higher quality data (Cumming et al., 2005), and writers of those high-rated written scripts are likely to be the language users with a higher proficiency level (Cumming, 1989; Weigle, 2002; Kim et al., 2018).

Complexity, accuracy and fluency are normally used to describe the quality of L2 learners' written production or performance (Taguchi et al., 2013; Barrot et al., 2021; Tabari et al., 2022), so they are usually considered as a significant indicator of L2 writing proficiency (Ortega, 2012; Barrot et al., 2021; Tabari et al., 2022). Complexity stands for learners' language sophistication in terms of grammatical forms and structures (Skehan, 2009; Pallotti, 2015). Accuracy refers to learners' ability to use language correctly both in form and structure (Skehan, 2009). Fluency is usually related to learners' ability to produce written words, clauses, as well as T-units (Ellis et al., 2005). As explained by Hunt (1970), the T-unit is considered as the main clause, while subordinate clauses and non-clausal structures are attached to or embedded in the main clause. Hence, it is reasonable to identify a better content alignment between Item 99 and Descriptor 5.

Descriptor 4 refers to the statement "can complete common narratives, expositions, and argumentations, etc. of no less than 450 Chinese characters in a limited time" involved in the writing sub-scales of the *Standards* Level 5 (Center for Language Education and Cooperation, 2021b). This descriptor describes learners' ability to write an article. The expected length, the text genres, as well as the topics have been mentioned.

With regard to the relatively unsatisfactory content alignment between Item 99 and Descriptor 4, the interview data provides tentative answers.

Interviewee A and Interviewee B have voluntarily participated in the interview. They put forward that compared with Descriptor 4, the requirements on expected text genres, are not stated clearly and directly in the instructions of Item 99, which leads to a relatively unsatisfactory content alignment, and they make the judgment by analyzing the words provided in Item 99.

Instead of being presented explicitly, the text genres that the instructions of Item 99 are intended to elicit are indicated by the provided words, which further confirms the results of previous studies. Biber (1988) stressed that the language of different types of writing, such as narrative and non-narrative writing, is different. Thus, it is reasonable to identify text genres by analyzing the linguistic features of texts. Since all the provided words should be used in examinees' written scripts, the features of those words can be used to identify the expected genres. As extracted from Interviewee A' replies, the words provided by Item 99 selected from 3 sets of HSK Level 5 sample test papers can lead to a narrative, an argumentation or an exposition.

However, Item 99 requires test takers to write an essay with the provided words, which leads to different kinds of topics and text genres owing to the free imagination of examinees. Furthermore, previous studies have suggested that learners perform differently on writing tasks in response to the change of genres, and their performance is usually better for narratives than for other genres (Kamberelis, 1999; Li, 2014). Thus, examinees are likely to write in the genre of which they have a better grasp. Specifically, they will give preference to narrative writing. In this sense, it is difficult to ensure that Item 99 can fully cover the requirements of expected genres made by the *Standards* Level 5, which serves as a reasonable explanation of the relatively unsatisfactory content alignment between Item 99 and Descriptor 4.

It should also be noticed that the basis on which Interviewee B makes her judgment is the difficulty of words provided in Item 99. In her opinion, if an examinee can master words and phrases of the advanced level, then the examinee is likely to have a relatively satisfactory grasp of writing in different genres, which is consistent with the assumption of previous studies.

Previous studies suggest that L2 learners' writing proficiency can be reflected by their language knowledge. As pointed out by Grabe et al. (1996), as well as Schoonen et al. (2011), L2 knowledge plays a crucial role in proficient L2 writing, because it enables L2 writers to transform propositional ideas into verbal forms. In addition, Kyle et al. (2016) have also mentioned that high-rated essays tend to include more sophisticated lexis. Thus, it is relatively reasonable to assume that learners of a higher proficiency level tend to master the words and phrases of the advanced level. Besides, as mentioned before, the change of genres has an influence on learners' performance, and writing narratives seem to be easier. To sum up, learners who have mastered sophisticated words and phrases are likely to be proficient L2 writers, and they tend to have a grasp of writing in different genres. Thus, it is relatively reasonable to make inferences based on the difficulty of words provided in Item 99.

In conclusion, Item 99 can be basically aligned with the *Standards* Level 5. However, the *Standards* Level 5 is more informative than Item 99 in terms of expected genres. Hence, there seems to be a need for test developers to enrich the instructions of Item 99, and the information of expected genres should be provided clearly and directly, so as to have a better degree of content alignment.

However, whether and how to enrich the information involved in the instructions of Item 99 remains a problem, which is closely related to the task difficulty. Considering the aim of promoting HSK worldwide, the difficulty of HSK should be controlled carefully, so as to encourage learners to make progress in learning Chinese language continually (Zhang et al., 2010; Luo et al., 2011). Specifically, the amount of information provided by the instructions affects candidates' load of identifying task requirements, and has an influence on the task difficulty (Weigle, 2002). In addition, the difficulty of a task is also affected by different genres elicited by the instructions. The participants of HSK have various social and cultural backgrounds, as well as different levels of language proficiency. Thus, if a specific genre is required by

Item 99, the methods of ensuring the appropriate difficulty and fairness of Item 99 will be a problem for test developers.

Furthermore, the present study does not take all writing tasks of HSK Level 5 into consideration. The coverage of text genres in the *Standards* cannot be fully reflected by a single writing task. In addition, experts' judgment is based on Items 99 and 100 selected from 3 sets of HSK Level 5 sample test papers. The selection of the sample test paper will definitely affect experts' judgment. To sum up, more evidence should be collected for a more specific and credible analysis.

10.1.2 The Content of Item 100

According to the results of descriptive analysis and binomial test, most experts think that Item 100 can be aligned with the *Standards* from the content perspective basically, which further verifies the results of the qualitative content analysis of *HSK Rating Criteria*, *HSK Test Syllabus* and *HSK Test Item-writing Manual*. Different from Item 99, the results of the one-way ANOVA show that there is no significant difference among experts' judgment on the alignment between Item 100 and each of the 6 descriptors. But the results of the post-hoc test show that the content alignment between Item 100 and Descriptor 3 is relatively unsatisfactory.

To unveil the reasons behind those findings, care should be taken to analyze the instructions of Item 100. The statement "please write a short article of about 80 Chinese characters based on the picture below" is provided as the instructions of Item 100 (Hanban, 2015).

A plausible explanation for the different results of the one-way ANOVA for Item 99 and Item 100 can be related to the different stimulus material provided by the two questions. The stimulus material of Item 99 is several words, while that of Item 100 is a picture. As discussed before, experts make the judgment mainly based on the words provide in Item 99. However, both Interviewee C and Interviewee D who voluntarily participate in the present study point out that their judgment is not affected by the picture, because the provided picture imposes nearly no restriction on candidates' writing. Based on the picture, candidates can write a short article on topics and genres they are familiar with, and they can use Chinese characters and sentence patterns they have already mastered. All we know for sure is that candidates need to write a short article, and the expected length is 80 Chinese characters. Thus, it brings difficulties in judging the extent to which Item 100 can cover the requirements of the *Standards* Level 5, which explains the reason why no significant difference exists among experts' judgment on the content alignment between Item 100 and each of the 6 descriptors.

As for the relatively unsatisfactory content alignment between Item 100 and Descriptor 3, there are two tentative answers extracted from the interview data. Descriptor 3 refers to the description "can analyze the structure of common Chinese characters" (Center for Language Education and Cooperation, 2021b).

First, the instructions of Item 100 ensure enough flexibility for candidates' writing. Candidates can choose to use Chinese characters they have already mastered in their writing. Besides, since the range of common Chinese characters has not been defined clearly by the *Standards*, it is difficult to judge whether Item 100 can cover the requirements of Descriptor 3.

Second, instead of describing learners' ability to write an article, Descriptor 3 focuses on the ability to analyze the structures of Chinese characters. A detailed definition of this ability has not been given. As mentioned by Interviewee D, whether it is reasonable to assume that candidates who can write Chinese characters with correct structures have this ability remains unsure. But in her opinion, the requirement for analyzing the structures of Chinese characters is higher than that for writing Chinese characters. Hence, it's really hard to make a content alignment between Item 100 and Descriptor 3.

In conclusion, Item 100 can basically be aligned with the *Standards* Level 5. To have a better degree of content alignment, requirements for learners' language knowledge should be stated clearly by the instructions of Item 100.

Besides, vague expressions should be avoided in the *Standards* as well. However, whether and how the test developers enrich the instructions depends on the construct of Item 100 of HSK Level 5. To promote HSK worldwide, the difficulty of Item 100 should be controlled carefully. Thus, test developers should be cautious enough.

Furthermore, a single task cannot represent HSK Level 5 writing test, and the selection of the sample tasks will definitely affect experts' judgment. Therefore, the result of the content alignment provided by the present study is only a reference. To have a more specific and credible result, more evidence should be collected.

10.2 Discussion on the Performance Standards

The preliminary results elicited by the content alignment will be corroborated in the step of standard setting. Usually, a performance standard is set to differentiate learners of different proficiency levels in this aligning step. In most aligning studies, the performance standard is the test scores of the borderline candidates who just meet the required proficiency level, which is always called the cut-off scores.

In this study, the answers to both Research Questions 3 and 4 are drawn from this aligning step. In other words, cut-off scores will be provided as the results of those two questions, so as to allocate HSK Level 5 test takers into two proficiency levels: Level 5 or Level 5 minus.

But the two questions differ from each other in terms of the different participants or judges involved, which explains the reason why the discussion on the performance standards will be further divided into two chapters. To answer Research Question 3, HSK Level 5 test takers are invited to make a self-evaluation of their writing ability according to the descriptors in the writing sub-scales of the *Standards* Level 5. To answer Research Question 4, experts are invited to judge the relation between HSK Level 5 test takers' written scripts of Items 99 and 100 and the descriptors in the writing sub-scales of the *Standards* Level 5.

The quantitative questionnaire survey is adopted to answer both Research Questions 3 and 4. To unveil the underlying factors which affect experts' judgment, 4 experts are invited to make comments on their judgment.

10.2.1 The Performance Standards Based on Examinees' Self-evaluation

The reliability of examinees' self-evaluation data is suggested by the relation of two groups of data: their self-evaluation data collected by questionnaires, and their actual HSK scores provided by the Center for Language Education and Cooperation.

To have an in-depth exploration, examinees are categorized according to their self-evaluation data and actual HSK scores. Moreover, since the present study only focuses on Item 99 and Item 100, the relation between examinees' self-evaluation data and their overall scores on Items 99 and 100, scores on Item 99, as well as scores on Item 100 is analyzed.

Firstly, based on their self-evaluation data, examinees are divided into two groups: Group 1 and Group 2. Members of Group 1 don't think that they can reach the requirements of the *Standards* Level 5, and the mean of their questionnaire options is less than or equals 3, while examinees of Group 2 deem that they can reach the requirements of the *Standards* Level 5, and the mean of their questionnaire options is higher than 3.

As indicated by the relation between examinees' questionnaire data and their overall scores on Items 99 and 100, only examinees of Group 2 can make a reliable self-evaluation. Because the Pearson correlation coefficient is 0.303, it also indicates the level of correlation. Then, the results between the regression analysis further point out that there is a significant positive linear relation between the two groups of data: the questionnaire data and overall scores. Hence, the two groups of data can predict each other.

As suggested by the relation between examinees' questionnaire data and their scores on Item 99, only the examinees of Group 2 can make a reliable self-evaluation. Because the Pearson correlation coefficient is 0.311, which indicates the level of correlation as well. Then, the results of the regression analysis further point out that there is a significant positive linear relation between the two groups of data: the questionnaire data and scores on Item 99. Thus, the two groups of data can predict each other.

But when it comes to the relation between the examinees' questionnaire data and their scores on Item 100, the results of the correlation analysis show that there exists no significant correlation. In other words, the self-evaluation data of the examinees of Group 2 and their scores on Item 100 cannot predict each other.

The performance standards or cut-off scores should be set to differentiate examinees to different proficiency levels on the basis of reliable self-evaluation data. The average test scores of the borderline examinees who just meet the required proficiency level are regarded as the cut-off scores. Thus, according to the self-evaluation data of examinees of Group 2, a group of borderline candidates are selected. The results show that examinees whose overall scores on Items 99 and 100 are at least 23.75, or scores on Item 99 are no less than 9.9 can be allocated to the *Standards* Level 5.

Secondly, based on their actual scores, examinees are classified into two groups again: the low-score group and the high-score group. The results of the correlation analysis show that the self-evaluation data of those getting a high score on Item 99 is not reliable. Only the examinees who gain a high score on Item 100 are able to evaluate their writing ability reasonably. The Pearson correlation coefficient is 0.251. Then, the results of the regression analysis further point out that there is a significant positive linear relation between the two groups of data: the self-evaluation questionnaire data of the the examinees who gain a high score on Item 100, and their scores on Item 100.

Similarly, according to the self-evaluation questionnaire data of the examinees who gains a high score on Item 100, a group of borderline candidates are selected. Their average score on Item 100 is regarded as the cut-off score. The results show that the cut-off score is 14.7, which means that the examinees whose scores on Question100 are higher than or equal to 14.7

can be allocated to the *Standards* Level 5.

In conclusion, the self-evaluation data of the examinees who consider themselves to reach the requirements of the *Standards* Level 5 can predict their overall scores on Items 99 and 100, as well as scores on Item 99. The self-evaluation data of the examinees who get a high score on Item 100 can show the predictive power to their scores on Item 100. However, the cut-off scores presented above only serve as a reference, since the cut-off scores are affected by the selection of sample examinees' scripts.

It should be noted that those findings also shed light on the difficulty of writing tasks in HSK Level 5 writing test. Specifically, Item 100 is more difficult than Item 99. Examinees having a good performance on Item 100 have the self-evaluation ability, while those having a good performance on Item 99 still cannot evaluate their writing ability.

10.2.2 The Performance Standards Based on Experts' Judgment

The results of the descriptive analysis reflect that Item 99 and Item 100 of HSK Level 5 writing test can basically be aligned with the *Standards* Level 5 from the perspective of the examinees' written scripts, which is in line with the answer to Research Question 3.

However, the results of the one-way ANOVA and post-hoc test show that there exists a relatively unsatisfactory alignment between the examinees' scripts and Descriptor 4. Interviewees' replies provide a plausible explanation of the finding.

As mentioned before, Descriptor 4 refers to the statement "can complete common narratives, expositions, and argumentations, etc. of no less than 450 Chinese characters in a limited time" involved in the writing sub-scales of the *Standards* Level 5 (Center for Language Education and Cooperation, 2021b). It makes requirements on learners' written scripts, especially the expected length and text genres.

In terms of the length of scripts, as extracted from interviewees' answers, no sample scripts can reach the requirements on the expected length made by Descriptor 4. Specifically, HSK Level 5 examinees only write a short article of about 80 Chinese characters, but Descriptor 4 requires learners to write an essay of 450 Chinese characters. The gap cannot be neglected.

As for the text genres, Descriptor 4 requires examinees to write narratives, expositions and argumentations. But the replies of interviewees show that since the text genre is not limited by the instructions, most examinees tend to write a narrative. Candidates always try their best to fully perform to the best of their abilities. They are likely to avoid writing in the genre they are not proficient in. In this sense, writing a narrative is much easier for candidates, and they may have more practice in narrative writing, which is consistent with the results of previous studies. Previous studies suggest that learners perform differently on writing tasks in response to the change of genres, and their performance is usually better for narratives than for other genres (Kamberelis, 1999; Li, 2014). Thus, examinees will give preference to narrative writings.

In conclusion, Item 99 and Item 100 can be basically aligned with the *Standards* Level 5 from the perspective of the examinees' written scripts. However, the *Standards* are more demanding in terms of the expected length and text genres. Hence, it seems necessary for HSK test developers to pose a higher requirement on the length and impose limitations on text genres. Besides, examinees' ability to write in different genres should be improved.

However, since the present study does not cover all writing tasks of HSK Level 5 writing test, and the selection of sample written scripts will affect experts' judgment, the results of this aligning study can only be considered as a reference.

Before setting performance standards based on experts' judgment, the reliability of experts' judgment should be analyzed. As reflected by the results of the correlation analysis, the experts' judgment is reliable, and the reliability of the experts' judgment is at a relatively satisfactory level. Specifically, the Pearson correlation coefficient of the experts' judgment and the examinees' scores on Item 99 is 0.704, and that of the experts' judgment and the examinees' scores on Item 100 is 0.602. When the correlation coefficient is higher than 0.6, it can be proved that a strong correlation exists between the two groups of data. Besides, the two groups of data are considered positively correlated if the correlation coefficient is larger than 0 (Tabachnick et al., 2014). Furthermore, the results of the regression analysis show that there exists a positive linear relation between the experts' judgment and the examinees' scores. Thus, it is reasonable to set performance standards or cut-off scores on the basis of the experts' judgment.

The average scores of the borderline examinees who just meet the required proficiency level are considered as cut-off scores. The results show that the examinees whose scores on Item 99 are at least 12, or scores on Item 100 are no less than 15 can be allocated to the *Standards* Level 5. As mentioned before, the cut-off scores provided in this study can only be a reference.

What is noteworthy is that the performance standards based on experts' judgment are more reliable than those based on examinees' self-evaluation. The experts' judgment on HSK Level 5 test takers' scripts is more reliable than examinees' self-evaluation of their writing ability, which is suggested by the Pearson correlation coefficient. In addition, the cut-off scores based on the experts' judgment are obviously higher than those based on the examinees' self-evaluation, which may result from the examinees' tendency of overestimating their writing ability. Hence, the examinees' self-evaluation ability needs to be improved.

11 Conclusion

The final chapter of this study comes to the conclusion. Firstly, the major findings of this study are summarized. Secondly, the implications of this study are provided. Finally, limitations and directions for future research are pointed out.

11.1 The Major Findings of the Present Study

In order to align HSK Level 5 writing test with the *Standards*, the present study is intended to use qualitative content analysis data, questionnaire data, interview data and HSK test scores to answer the four research questions. First, from the content perspective, this study explores (1) What is the relation between *HSK Rating Criteria*, *HSK Test Syllabus* and *HSK Test Item-Writing Manual* for Items 99 and 100 of HSK Level 5, and the *Standards*? (2) To what extent can Items 99 and 100 of HSK Level 5 cover the requirements of the *Standards*? Then, from the perspective on examinees' actual performance, this study tries to answer: (3) What is the relation between examinees' self-evaluation of their writing abilities based on the *Standards* and their actual scores on Items 99 and 100 of HSK Level 5? (4) To what extent can Items 99 and 100 of HSK Level 5 be related with the *Standards*?

To begin with, the content of *HSK Rating Criteria*, *HSK Test Syllabus* and *HSK Test Item-Writing Manual* for Items 99 and 100 can be matched with that of the *Standards* Level 5 in terms of the communicative context, communicative functions, quantitative criteria and the quality of produced texts. It indicates the possibility of the content alignment, and the feasibility of this aligning study.

Secondly, Items 99 and 100 of HSK Level 5 writing test can basically cover the requirements of the *Standards* Level 5 from the content perspective, but there still exists room for improvement. Specifically, the *Standards* is more informative in terms of the requirements on text genres and learners' language knowledge. In this sense, it seems necessary for HSK test developers to enrich the information involved in the instructions of Items 99 and 100 and make the requirements on examinees' performance clearer, so as to have a better degree of the content alignment. However, considering the aim of promoting HSK worldwide, the difficulty of HSK should be controlled carefully. Thus, whether and how to enrich the information involved in the instructions remains a problem. In addition, it should be noted that the vague expressions involved in the *Standards* can also be obstacles to the alignment between HSK and the *Standards*. Hence, descriptors in the *Standards* should be expressed without ambiguity.

Thirdly, the self-evaluation of the examinees who consider that they can meet the requirements of the *Standards* Level 5 is positively correlated with their overall scores on Items 99 and 100, and scores on Item 99. Besides, the self-evaluation of those who get a high score on Item 100 is also positively correlated with their scores on Item 100. The correlations are all significant, but at a low level. Item 100 is more difficult than Item 99, and the examinees' self-evaluation ability should be improved. Based on the examinees' self-evaluation, the examinees whose overall scores on Items 99 and 100 are at least 23.75, scores on Item 99 are no less than 9.9, or scores on Item 100 are at least 14.7, can be allocated to the *Standards* Level 5 in terms of Chinese writing proficiency.

Fourthly, HSK Level 5 writing test can basically be aligned with the *Standards* Level 5 from the perspective of examinees' actual performance. But HSK Level 5 examinees' written scripts cannot fully reflect the requirements of the *Standards*. To be specific, the *Standards* is more demanding in terms of the expected length and text genres. And it seems necessary for HSK test developers to sample more on the length and impose limitations on text genres. Besides, the examinees' ability to write in genres other than the narrative style should be sampled and improved. The strong and positive correlations between the experts' judgment and the actual HSK scores of examinees indicates that the experts' judgment is more reliable than the examinees' self-evaluation. Based on the experts' judgment, the examinees whose scores on Item 99 are no less than 12, or scores on Item 100 are at least 15 can be allocated to the *Standards* Level 5 as far as their Chinese writing ability is considered.

Q1: What is the relation between *HSK Rating Criteria*, *HSK Test Syllabus* and *HSK Test Item-Writing Manual* for Items 99 and 100 of HSK Level 5, and the *Standards*?

The content of *HSK Rating Criteria*, *HSK Test Syllabus* and *HSK Test Item-Writing Manual* for Items 99 and 100 can be matched with that of the *Standards* Level 5.

Q2: To what extent can Items 99 and 100 of HSK Level 5 cover the requirements of the *Standards*?

1) Items 99 and 100 of HSK Level 5 can basically cover the requirements of the *Standards* Level 5 from the content perspective.

2) The *Standards* are more informative in terms of the requirements on text genres and learners' language knowledge.

Q3: What is the relation between examinees' self-evaluation of their writing abilities based on the *Standards*, and their actual scores on Items 99 and 100 of HSK Level 5?

1) The self-evaluation of examinees who consider that they can meet the requirements of the *Standards* Level 5 is positively correlated with their overall scores on Items 99 and 100, and scores on Item 99.

2) The self-evaluation of those who get a high score on Item 100 is also positively correlated with their scores on Item 100.

3) The correlations are all significant, but at a low level.

4) The examinees whose overall scores on Items 99 and 100 are at least

23.75, scores on Item 99 are no less than 9.9, or scores on Item 100 are at least 14.7 can be allocated to the *Standards* Level 5.

Q4: To what extent can Items 99 and 100 of HSK Level 5 be related with the *Standards*?

1) HSK Level 5 writing test can basically be aligned with the *Standards* Level 5 from the perspective of examinees' actual performance.

2) The *Standards* is more demanding in terms of the expected length and text genres.

3) The examinees whose scores on Item 99 are no less than 12, or scores on Item 100 are at least 15 can be allocated to the *Standards* Level 5.

11.2　Implications of the Present Study

The findings of this aligning study contribute to language testing, as well as language education.

In the field of language testing, the present study is enlightening in terms of the methods of the content alignment and the standard setting. In terms of the content alignment, materials related to the construct of HSK Level 5 writing test, including *HSK Rating Criteria*, *HSK Test Syllabus* and *HSK Test Item-Writing Manual*, as well as sample test papers, have been analyzed in relation to the *Standards* Level 5. In the step of standard setting, performance standards are set on the basis of both examinees' self-evaluation and experts' judgment.

In addition, the findings of this study are also insightful and thought-provoking in terms of the reform of HSK and the refinement of the *Standards*. Specifically, vague expressions should be avoided in the *Standards*, and it seems necessary for HSK test developers to enrich the instructions of Items 99 and 100 and make the wording of instructions more explicit. Although Item 100 is more difficult than Item 99, the difficulty of both Item 99 and Item 100 should be improved. However, considering the aim of promoting HSK worldwide, the difficulty of HSK should be controlled carefully.

In the field of language education, the findings of the present study are of great significance. Firstly, HSK Level 5 examinees' ability to write in genres other than the narrative style, as well as their ability to write a lengthy article needs to be improved. Besides, the examinees' self-evaluation ability should also be improved. Secondly, this aligning study provides a more transparent interpretation of HSK test results, which is beneficial for the users of HSK test results and the test takers themselves. To be specific, it will be much easier for test takers to know their actual Chinese proficiency based on the *Standards*, and Chinese language teachers can have a clear grasp of students' Chinese proficiency. Policymakers who set language proficiency requirements can also have a better understanding of HSK test results, and then make more reasonable policies.

11.3 Limitations and Directions for Further Research

Firstly, since the whole aligning procedure provided in the *Manual* is too time-consuming, the present study makes an adaption. To make a content alignment, materials related to the construct of HSK Level 5 writing test have been analyzed in relation to the *Standards*. In this step, the selection of HSK Level 5 sample test papers affects the results of the content alignment. In addition, only 3 sets of sample test papers have been chosen. Then, in terms of the performance standards provided in the present study, they are based on both the examinees' self-evaluation and the experts' judgment. The selection of examinees and their written scripts of Items 99 and 100 have a great influence on the performance standards. Besides, when setting performance standards, socio-cultural factors should also be taken into consideration. To sum up, the aligning results provided in this study only serve as a reference.

Secondly, the writing sub-scales of the *Standards* divide test takers' writing ability into 6 levels. Different from other aligning research, the present study aligns HSK Level 5 with the descriptors in the writing sub-scales of the *Standards* Level 5 only. For a more specific aligning result, descriptors of adjacent levels should be covered in future studies.

Thirdly, although the Center for Language Education and Cooperation have provided an official explanation of the theoretical grounding and underlying structure of the *Standards*, the structure of descriptors in the writing sub-scales hasn't been introduced in detail. A more accurate explanation needs to be provided, which will benefit future aligning studies a lot.

References:

白小丽,李孟语(Bai X L, Li M Y.),2017. 应试目标下的 HSK 五级关键词写作试题分析及教学建议[J]. 云南师范大学学报(对外汉语教学与研究版),15(6):11 – 27.

陈明(Chen M),2018. HSK 五级听力测试的真实性考察[J]. 现代语文（5）:175 – 180.

成波(Cheng B),2011. 汉语能力标准与欧洲及加拿大语言能力标准比较研究[D]. 长沙:湖南大学.

方绪军(Fang X J),2007. CEFR 对汉语测试研发的启示[J]. 世界汉语教学,21(2):136 – 143.

符华均,张晋军,李亚男,等(Fu H J, Zhang J J, Li Y N, et al),2013. 新汉语水平考试 HSK(五级)效度研究[J]. 考试研究,9（3）:65 – 69.

韩宝成(Han B C),2006. 国外语言能力量表述评[J]. 外语教学与研究,38(6):443 – 450.

汉办(Hanban),2015. HSK 五级考试大纲[M]. 北京:人民教育出版社.

汉考国际(Chinese Testing International),2021. HSK3.0 研发专家意见征询会纪要[J]. 世界汉语教学,35（3）:432.

何莲珍(He L Z),2019. 语言考试与语言标准对接的效度验证框架[J]. 现代外语,42(5):660 – 671.

何莲珍,罗蓝(He L Z, Luo L),2020. 语言考试与语言能力量表对接研究:路径与方法[J]. 外语教学,41(1):29 – 33.

黄婷，贾国栋(Huang T, Jia G D)，2012. 语言测试与《欧洲语言共同参考框架》匹配的可行性研究：以大学英语四、六级考试为例[J]. 外语测试与教学(1)：38-49.

教育部中外语言交流合作中心(Center for Language Education and Cooperation)，2021a. 国际中文教育中文水平等级标准[S/OL]. http://www.moe.gov.cn/jyb_xwfb/gzdt_gzdt/s5987/202103/t20210329_523304.html.

教育部中外语言交流合作中心(Center for Language Education and Cooperation)，2021b. 国际中文教育中文水平等级标准(国家标准·应用解读本)[M]. 北京：北京语言大学出版社.

李曼丽，李加鏊(Li M L, Li J P)，2020. 国内外语言能力量表的描述语特征分析[J]. 中国考试(6)：36-42.

李绍山(Li S S)，2001. 语言研究中的统计学[M]. 西安：西安交通大学出版社.

李行健(Li X J)，2021. 一部全新的立足汉语特点的国家等级标准：谈《国际中文教育中文水平等级标准》的研制与应用[J]. 国际汉语教学研究(1)：8-11.

刘建达(Liu J D)，2015. 我国英语能力等级量表研制的基本思路[J]. 中国考试(1)：7-11.

刘建达，韩宝成(Liu J D, Han B C)，2018. 面向运用的中国英语能力等级量表建设的理论基础[J]. 现代外语，41(1)：78-90.

刘书慧(Liu S H)，2014. 以内省法检验新HSK五级完型填空的效度：基于反应过程的证据[J]. 华南师范大学学报(社会科学版)(2)：142-146.

刘英林(Liu Y L)，1989. 汉语水平考试(HSK)的基本模式[J]. 语言教学与研究(1)：84-94.

刘英林(Liu Y L)，1994. 汉语水平考试(HSK)的理论基础探讨[J]. 汉语学习(1)：40-48.

刘英林，李佩泽，李亚男(Liu Y, Li P Z, Li Y N.)，2020. 汉语国际教育汉语水平等级标准全球化之路[J]. 世界汉语教学，34(2)：147-157.

刘英林，郭树军，王志芳(Liu Y L, Guo S J, Wang Z F)，1988. 汉语水平考试(HSK)的性质和特点[J]. 世界汉语教学(2)：110-120.

卢晓，余瑾(Lu X, Yu J)，2012. 基于新五级HSK初中级过渡期综合课中的语段写作训练探索[J]. 教育与教学研究,26(10):77-80.

鹿士义(Lu S Y),2011b. 商务汉语考试(BCT)与欧洲语言共同参考框架(CEFR)的等级标准关系研究[J]. 华文教学与研究(2):56-63.

鹿士义(Lu S Y),2011a. 商务汉语考试(BCT)阅读能力与欧盟框架的匹配研究[J]. 语言文字应用(1):81-90.

罗莲(Luo L),2017. 汉语分级测试与CEFR等级的连接研究[J]. 语言文字应用(2):110-118.

罗民,张晋军,谢欧航,等(Luo M,Zhang J J,Xie O H,et al.),2011a. 新汉语水平考试(HSK)质量报告[J]. 中国考试(10):3-7.

罗民,张晋军,谢欧航,等(Luo M,Zhang J J,Xie O H,et al),2011b. 新汉语水平考试(HSK)海外实施报告[J]. 中国考试(4):17-21.

闵尚超,姜子芸(Min S C,Jiang Z Y),2020. 校本听力考试与《中国英语能力等级量表》对接研究[J]. 外语教学,41(4):47-51.

Papageorgiou S,刘洋(Papageorgiou S,Liu Y),2019. 考试测评与语言能力标准对接中的若干问题[J]. 中国考试(8):1-7+20.

彭川(Peng C.),2021.《中国英语能力等级量表》与《欧洲语言共同参考框架》的级别对接研究:以写作能力为例[J]. 外语界(5):84-93.

彭川,刘建达(Peng C,Liu J D),2021.《中国英语能力等级量表》与《欧洲语言共同参考框架》听力技能级别对接研究[J]. 外语教学,42(5):43-50.

盛炎(Sheng Y),1988.《汉语水平等级标准和等级大纲(试行)》与国外一些标准和大纲的比较[J]. 世界汉语教学,2(4):241-243.

王伯韬(Wang B T),(2015). 英语专业四、八级考试与《欧洲语言共同参考框架》对接的可行性研究[D]. 扬州:扬州大学.

王华(Wang H),2020. 校本英语水平考试与《中国英语能力等级量表》的对接研究:以"上海交通大学英语水平考试"为例[J]. 外语界(5):72-79.

谢小庆(Xie X Q),2011. 为什么要开发新HSK考试?[J]. 中国考试(3):10-13.

张晋军,解妮妮,王世华,等(Zhang J J,Xie N N,Wang S H,et al),2010. 新汉语水平考试(HSK)研制报告[J]. 中国考试(9):38-43.

张晋军,邱宁,张洁(Zhang J J,Qiu N,Zhang J),2009. 汉语水平考试与《国际汉语能力标准》挂钩研究报告[J]. 中国考试(4):18-24.

张新玲,黄泳(Zhang X L, Huang Y),2021. 英美、日韩考生 HSK 5 级"规定词书写"题文本特征研究[J]. 汉语教学学刊 (13)：95－110＋156.

张新生(Zhang X S),2021.《欧洲语言共同参考框架》与国际汉语水平等级标准[J]. 国际中文教育(中英文) 6(2)：65－73.

张新生,李明芳(Zhang X S, Li M F),2019. 汉语能力标准比较初探[J]. 国际汉语教学研究 (1)：31－47.

赵琪凤(Zhao Q F),2016. 汉语水平考试的历史回顾及研究述评[J]. 中国考试 (9)：47－53.

周碧(Zhou B),2020. 高考英语阅读(NMET)与中国英语能力等级量表(CSE)的匹配研究[D]. 广州：广东外语外贸大学.

邹申(Zou S),1998. 英语语言测试：理论与操作[M]. 上海：上海外语教育出版社.

邹申,张文星,孔菊芳(Zou S, Zhang W X, Kong J F),2015.《欧洲语言共同参考框架》在中国：研究现状与应用展望[J]. 中国外语,12(3)：24－31.

American Council on the Teaching of Foreign Languages，2012. ACTFL Proficiency Guidelines ［S/OL］. 2022－3. https://www.actfl.org/resources/actfl-proficiency-guidelines-2012.

American Educational Research Association，American Psychological Association，National Council on Measurement in Education，2005. Standards for educational and psychological testing [M]. Washington, DC：American Educational Research Association.

Bachman L F, 1990. Fundamental considerations in language testing [M]. Oxford：Oxford University Press.

Bachman L F, Spolsky B, 1995. An investigation into the comparability of two tests of English as a foreign language [M]. Cambridge：Cambridge University Press.

Barrot J S, Agdeppa J Y,2021. Complexity, accuracy and fluency as indices of college-level L2 writers' proficiency[J]. Assessing writing, 47：100510.

Bechger T M, Kuijper H, Maris G,2009. Standard setting in relation to the common European framework of reference for languages：The case of the state examination of Dutch as a second language[J]. Language assessment quarterly, 6(2): 126-150.

Biber D, 1988. Validation across speech and writing [M]. Cambridge: Cambridge University Press.

Canale M, Swain M, 1980. Theoretical bases of communicative approaches to second language teaching and testing[J]. Applied linguistics, I(1): 1-47.

Chen X L, Hu J E, 2020. Going global: The successful link of IELTS and aptis to China's standards of English language ability (CSE) [J]. International journal of English linguistics, 11(1): 1-9.

Chomsky N, 1965. Aspects of the Theory of Syntax [M]. Cambridge: The MIT Press.

Cizek G J, 2001. Setting performance standards: Concepts, methods and perspectives [M]. Mahwah, NJ: Lawrence Erlbaum Associates.

Council of Europe, 2001. Common European framework of reference for languages: Learning, teaching, assessment [M]. Cambridge: Cambridge University Press.

Council of Europe, 2009. Relating language examinations to the common European framework of reference for languages: Learning, teaching, assessment (CEFR): A manual [M]. Strasbourg: Council of Europe, Language Policy Division.

Cumming A, 1989. Writing expertise and second-language proficiency[J]. Language learning, 3(1): 81-135.

Cumming A, Kantor R, Baba K, et al, 2005. Differences in written discourse in independent and integrated prototype tasks for next generation TOEFL [J]. Assessing Writing, 10(1): 5-43.

Davies A, Brown A, Elder C, et al, 2002. Dictionary of language testing [M]. Beijing: Foreign Language Teaching and Research Press.

Dunlea J, Spiby R, Wu S, et al, 2019. China's standards of English language ability (CSE): Linking UK exams to the CSE [R]. Manchester: British Council.

Ellis R, Barkhuizen G, 2005. Analysing learner language [M]. Oxford: Oxford University Press.

Figueras N, North B, Takala S, et al, 2005. Relating examinations to the Common European Framework: A manual[J]. Language Testing, 22(3): 261-279.

Fleckenstein J, Keller S, Krüger M, et al, 2020. Linking TOEFL iBT® writing rubrics to CEFR levels: Cut scores and validity evidence from a standard setting study[J]. Assessing Writing, 43: 100420.

Grabe W, Kaplan R B, 1996. Theory and practice of writing [M]. New York: Longman.

Grazyna P S, 2000. Canadian language benchmarks 2000: English, a second language for adults [M]. Ottawa: Center of Canadian Language Benchmarks.

Green A, 2018. Linking tests of English for academic purposes to the CEFR: The score user's perspective[J]. Language assessment quarterly, 15(1): 59-74.

Hambleton R K, 2001. Setting performance standards on educational assessments and criteria for evaluating the process [M]// Cizek G J. Setting performance standards: Concepts, methods and perspectives. Mahwah, NJ: Lawrence Erlbaum Publishers: 89-116.

Harsch C, Hartig J, 2015 What are we aligning tests to when we report test alignment to the CEFR? [J]. Language assessment quarterly, 12(4): 333-362.

Harsch C, Kanistra V P, 2020. Using an innovative standard-setting approach to align integrated and independent writing tasks to the CEFR [J]. Language assessment quarterly, 17(3): 262-281.

Hayes J R, Flower L S, 1980. Identifying the organization of writing processes [M]// Gregg L W, Steinberg E R. Cognitive processes in writing. Hillsdale, NJ: Lawrence Erlbaum Associates: 3-30.

Hayes J R, 1996. A new framework for understanding cognition and affect in writing [M]// Levy C M, Ransdell S. The science of writing: Theories, methods, individual differences and application. New York: Routledge.

Hidri S, 2021. Linking the International English language competency assessment suite of examinations to the common European framework of reference [J/OL]. Language testing in Asia, 11 (1): 1 - 24. https://doi. org/10. 1186/s40468 - 021 - 00123 - 8.

Hunt K W, 1970. Syntactic maturity in schoolchildren and adults [J]. Monographs of the society for research in child development, 35(1): iii.

Hymes D H, 1972. On communicative competence [M]// Pride J B, Holmes J. Sociolinguistics. Harmondsworth: Penguin: 269 - 293.

Interagency Round Table, 1985. ILR skill level descriptions [S]. Washington, D C: IRT.

Jaeger R M, 1989. Certification of student competence [R]// Linn R L. Educational measurement. Washington, D C: American Council on Education: 485 - 511.

Kaftandjieva F, 2004. Standard setting [M]// Council of Europe. Reference supplement to the Manual for Relating Language Examinations to the CEFR. Strasbourg, France: Language Policy Division: 1 - 43.

Kamberelis G, 1999. Genre development and learning: Children writing stories, science reports and poems [J]. Research in the teaching of English, 33 (4): 403 - 460.

Kane M, 1998. Choosing between examinee-centered and test-centered standard-setting methods[J]. Educational Assessment, 5(3): 129 - 145.

Khalifa H, Ffrench A, 2009. Aligning Cambridge ESOL Examinations to the CEFR: Issues & practice [J]. Cambridge ESOL Research Notes, 37: 10 - 14.

Kim M, Crossley S A, 2018. Modeling second language writing quality: A structural equation investigation of lexical, syntactic and cohesive features in source-based and independent writing[J]. Assessing writing, 37: 39 - 56.

Knoch U, 2009. Diagnostic writing assessment: The development and validation of a rating scale [M]. Frankfurt: Perter Lang.

Kolen M J, Brennan R L, 2004. Test equating, scaling and linking: Methods and practices [M]. 2nd ed. New York: Springer.

Kyle K, Crossley S, 2016. The relationship between lexical sophistication and independent and source-based writing [J]. Journal of second language writing, 34: 12 - 24.

Lee O, 2018. English language proficiency standards aligned with content standards[J]. Educational Researcher, 47(5): 317-327.

Li J L, 2014. Examining genre effects on test takers' summary writing performance[J]. Assessing Writing, 22: 75-90.

National Education Examinations Authority, 2018. China's standards of English language ability [S/OL]. (2022-04-16) http://www.moe.gov.cn/srcsite/A19/s229/201804/t20180416_333315.html.

Newton P, 2010. Thinking about linking[J]. Measurement: Interdisciplinary research & perspective, 8(1): 38-56.

North B, 2003. Scales for rating language performance: Descriptive models, formulation styles and presentation formats [R]. Princeton: Educational Testing Service.

Ortega L, 2012. Interlanguage complexity: A construct in search of theoretical renewal [M]// Kortmann B, Szmrecsanyi B. Linguistic complexity: Second language acquisition, indigenization, contact. Berlin: De Gruyter: 127-155.

Pallotti G, 2015. A simple view of linguistic complexity[J]. Second language research, 31(1): 117-134.

Papageorgiou S, Tannenbaum R J, Bridgeman B, et al, 2015. The association between TOEFL iBT® test scores and the common European framework of reference (CEFR) levels [R]. Princeton, NJ: Educational Testing Service.

Papageorgiou S, Wu S, Hsieh C N, et al, 2019. Mapping the TOEFL iBT® test scores to China's standards of English language ability: Implications for score interpretation and use[J]. ETS Research Report Series (1): 1-49.

Peng C, Liu J D, Cai H W, 2022. Aligning China's standards of English language ability with the common European framework of reference for languages[J]. The Asia-Pacific education researcher, 31(6): 667-677.

Schoonen R, van Gelderen A, Stoel R D, et al, 2011. Modeling the development of L1 and EFL writing proficiency of secondary school students [J]. Language learning, 61(1): 31-79.

Skehan P, 2009. Modelling second language performance: Integrating complexity, accuracy, fluency and lexis[J]. Applied linguistics, 30(4): 510-532.

Tabachnick B G, Fidell L S,2014. Using multivariate statistics[M]. Harlow: Pearson.

Tabari M A, Wang Y, 2022. Assessing linguistic complexity features in L2 writing: Understanding effects of topic familiarity and strategic planning within the realm of task readiness [J]. Assessing writing, 52: 1-14.

Taguchi N, Crawford W, Wetzel D Z, 2013. What linguistic features are indicative of writing quality? A case of argumentative essays in a college composition program[J]. TESOL quarterly, 47(2): 420-430.

Tannenbaum R J, Wylie E C, 2008. Linking English-language test scores onto the common European framework of reference: An application of standard-setting methodology[R]. Princeton, NJ: Educational Testing Service.

Tannenbaum R J, Cho Y, 2014. Critical factors to consider in evaluating standard-setting studies to map language test scores to frameworks of language proficiency[J]. Language assessment quarterly, 11(3): 233-249.

Weigle S C, 2002. Assessing Writing[M]. Cambridge, UK: Cambridge University Press.

Woods A, Fletcher P, Hughes A, 2000. Statistics in Language Studies [M]. Beijing: Foreign Language Teaching and Research Press.

第二部分：Aligning HSK Level 5 Writing Test with *Chinese Proficiency Grading Standards for International Chinese Language Education*

Appendices

Appendix A

《国际中文教育中文水平等级标准》学生问卷(5级)

A Questionnaire of *Chinese Proficiency Grading Standards for International Chinese Language Education*（Level 5）

(写作部分)

亲爱的同学：
Dear students：

  我们热情邀请您参加针对《国际中文教育中文水平等级标准》的问卷调查。该问卷需要您结合自己的**中文能力**，认真填写题目。问卷并非测试，答案没有对错之分，请根据您的实际情况作答。该问卷仅用作研究目的，我们会对您的个人信息及作答情况严格保密，请放心。非常感谢您的参与！

  We warmly invite you to participate in a questionnaire survey on *Chinese Proficiency Grading Standards for International Chinese Language Education*. This questionnaire requires you to carefully answer questions based on your Chinese proficiency. The questionnaire is not a test and the answers are not a matter of true or false. Please finish it according to your own situation. The questionnaire is set up for research purposes only. You can be assured that we will strictly keep your personal information and answers confidential. Thank you very much for your participation!

  下面您将看到一些有关《国际中文教育中文水平等级标准》的描述语，请认真阅读，在每个句子下面的数字中选出最能代表自己情况的相应数字，并且在**问卷答题卡**上将所选数字涂黑。数字的含义如下：

Below you will see some descriptors about *Chinese Proficiency Grading Standards for International Chinese Language Education*. Please read it carefully, and select the corresponding number that best represents your situation from the numbers below each sentence. Besides, you need to black out the corresponding number on your *Answer Sheet*.

1. 我能分析常见汉字的结构。

    □0 完全不符合　□1 勉强符合　□2 基本符合　□3 比较符合
    □4 完全符合

    I can analyze the structure of commonly occurring Chinese characters.

    □0 totally untrue　□1 hardly true　□2 basically true
    □3 largely true　□4 totally true

2. 我能在规定时间内,使用较为复杂的句式进行书面的语段表达,完成一般的叙述、说明或简单的议论性语言材料,字数不低于450字。

    □0 完全不符合　□1 勉强符合　□2 基本符合　□3 比较符合
    □4 完全符合

    I can use comparatively complex sentence patterns to write paragraphs, and complete common narrative, expository and simple argumentative language materials of no less than 450 Chinese characters in a limited time.

    □0 totally untrue　□1 hardly true　□2 basically true
    □3 largely true　□4 totally true

3. 我能在规定时间内,完成一般的叙述、说明或简单的议论性语言材料,用词较为恰当。

    □0 完全不符合　□1 勉强符合　□2 基本符合　□3 比较符合
    □4 完全符合

    I can complete common narrative, expository and simple argumentative language materials, with comparatively appropriate vocabulary, in a limited time in Chinese.

    □0 totally untrue　□1 hardly true　□2 basically true
    □3 largely true　□4 totally true

4. 我能在规定时间内,完成一般的叙述、说明或简单的议论性语言材料,句式基本正确。

    □0 完全不符合　□1 勉强符合　□2 基本符合　□3 比较符合
    □4 完全符合

I can complete common narrative, expository and simple argumentative language materials, with basically correct sentence patterns, in a limited time in Chinese.

☐0 totally untrue   ☐1 hardly true   ☐2 basically true   ☐3 largely true
☐4 totally true

5. 我能在规定时间内,完成一般的叙述、说明或简单的议论性语言材料,内容比较完整。

   ☐0 完全不符合   ☐1 勉强符合   ☐2 基本符合   ☐3 比较符合
   ☐4 完全符合

   I can complete common narrative, expository and simple argumentative language materials, with comparatively complete content, in a limited time in Chinese.

   ☐0 totally untrue   ☐1 hardly true   ☐2 basically true   ☐3 largely true
   ☐4 totally true

6. 我能在规定时间内,完成一般的叙述、说明或简单的议论性语言材料,表达比较清楚。

   ☐0 完全不符合   ☐1 勉强符合   ☐2 基本符合   ☐3 比较符合
   ☐4 完全符合

   I can complete common narrative, expository and simple argumentative language materials, with comparatively clear expression, in a limited time in Chinese.

   ☐0 totally untrue   ☐1 hardly true   ☐2 basically true
   ☐3 largely true   ☐4 totally true

7. 我能完成一般的应用文体写作,格式基本正确。

   ☐0 完全不符合   ☐1 勉强符合   ☐2 基本符合   ☐3 比较符合
   ☐4 完全符合

   I can complete common practical forms of writing with basically correct format in Chinese.

   ☐0 totally untrue   ☐1 hardly true   ☐2 basically true
   ☐3 largely true   ☐4 totally true

8. 我能完成一般的应用文体写作,表达基本规范。

    □0 完全不符合　□1 勉强符合　□2 基本符合　□3 比较符合
    □4 完全符合

    I can write common practical forms of writing with basically standard expression in Chinese.

    □0 totally untrue　□1 hardly true　□2 basically true
    □3 largely true　□4 totally true

9. 我能在规定时间内,使用语段完成简单的叙述和说明,字数不低于 300 字。

    □0 完全不符合　□1 勉强符合　□2 基本符合　□3 比较符合
    □4 完全符合

    I can write paragraphs to complete simple narratives and expositions of no less than 300 Chinese characters in a limited time.

    □0 totally untrue　□1 hardly true　□2 basically true
    □3 largely true　□4 totally true

10. 我能在规定时间内,完成常见的多种应用文体的书面表达,字数不低于 600 字。

    □0 完全不符合　□1 勉强符合　□2 基本符合　□3 比较符合
    □4 完全符合

    I can write various common practical forms of writing of no less than 600 Chinese characters in a limited time.

    □0 totally untrue　□1 hardly true　□2 basically true
    □3 largely true　□4 totally true

Appendix B
《国际中文教育中文水平等级标准》与 HSK 考题的关系判断问卷

尊敬的专家老师：

您好！非常感谢您拨冗参与此次研究！

如您所知，HSK 是一项国际化考试，重点考查母语非中文者运用中文进行交际的能力。于 2021 年 3 月正式发布的《国际中文教育中文水平等级标准》是我国首个面向外国中文学习者，全面描绘评价学习者中文语言技能和水平的规范标准。

请您运用您的专业知识，认真仔细阅读，完成本问卷中的判断。非常感谢您的合作和帮助。

请您仔细阅读以下内容：

一、数据保密原则：未经本研究负责人同意，不得以泄露、告知、公布、发表、出版、传授、转让或其他任何方式，直接或间接、故意或无意使第三方（非本研究受试）知悉本研究所提供的任何数据及材料；也不得未经本研究负责人同意，随意挪用本研究中所提供的数据和材料。

二、个人信息保护原则：您所填写的相关信息仅用作研究目的，我们不会对外披露任何有关您的个人资料与信息。

我已经阅读了本知情同意书和数据保密协议，理解本研究的数据保密要求，愿意参加此次研究。

受试签名：_____

本问卷列出了：

（1）3 套 HSK 5 级考题"书写"部分第 99 题和第 100 题真题；

（2）《国际中文教育中文水平等级标准》5 级写作描述语（已拆分）。

请您运用自己的专业知识，对下列写作题目在多大程度上能够取样（考察）《国际中文教育中文水平等级标准》5 级所描述的相应写作能力做出判断，并点击相应的数字。

第一套考题
（仅提供第 99 和第 100 题）

第 99 题：

请结合下列词语（要全部使用，顺序不分先后），写一篇 80 字左右的短文。

相处　往往　各自　矛盾　愉快

请判断上题，在多大程度上能够考查《国际中文教育中文水平等级标准》5 级所描述的相应写作能力，并点击相应的数字。

1. 能够掌握中等手写汉字表中的汉字 250 个。
   □1 完全不符合　□2 勉强符合　□3 基本符合　□4 比较符合
   □5 完全符合

2. 能够使用较为复杂的句式进行语段表达。
   □1 完全不符合　□2 勉强符合　□3 基本符合　□4 比较符合
   □5 完全符合

3. 能够分析常见汉字的结构。
   □1 完全不符合　□2 勉强符合　□3 基本符合　□4 比较符合
   □5 完全符合

4. 在规定时间内，完成一般的叙述性、说明性及简单的议论性等语言材料的写作，字数不低于 450 字。
   □1 完全不符合　□2 勉强符合　□3 基本符合　□4 比较符合
   □5 完全符合

5. 用词较为恰当，句式基本正确，内容比较完整，表达较为通顺。
   □1 完全不符合　□2 勉强符合　□3 基本符合　□4 比较符合
   □5 完全符合

6. 能够完成一般的应用文体写作，格式正确，表达基本规范。
   □1 完全不符合　□2 勉强符合　□3 基本符合　□4 比较符合
   □5 完全符合

第 100 题：

请结合这张图片写一篇 80 字左右的短文。

请判断上题,在多大程度上能够考查《国际中文教育中文水平等级标准》5级所描述的相应写作能力,并点击相应的数字。

7. 能够掌握中等手写汉字表中的汉字 250 个。

　　□1 完全不符合　　□2 勉强符合　　□3 基本符合　　□4 比较符合
　　□5 完全符合

8. 能够使用较为复杂的句式进行语段表达。

　　□1 完全不符合　　□2 勉强符合　　□3 基本符合　　□4 比较符合
　　□5 完全符合

9. 能够分析常见汉字的结构。

　　□1 完全不符合　　□2 勉强符合　　□3 基本符合　　□4 比较符合
　　□5 完全符合

10. 在规定时间内,完成一般的叙述性、说明性及简单的议论性等语言材料的写作,字数不低于 450 字。

　　□1 完全不符合　　□2 勉强符合　　□3 基本符合　　□4 比较符合
　　□5 完全符合

11. 用词较为恰当,句式基本正确,内容比较完整,表达较为通顺。

　　□1 完全不符合　　□2 勉强符合　　□3 基本符合　　□4 比较符合
　　□5 完全符合

12. 能够完成一般的应用文体写作,格式正确,表达基本规范。

　　□1 完全不符合　　□2 勉强符合　　□3 基本符合　　□4 比较符合
　　□5 完全符合

第二套考题
（仅提供第 99 和 100 题）

第 99 题：

请结合下列词语（要全部使用，顺序不分先后），写一篇 80 字左右的短文。

项链　　至今　　微笑　　浪漫　　母亲

请判断上题，在多大程度上能够考查《国际中文教育中文水平等级标准》5 级所描述的相应写作能力，并点击相应的数字。

13. 能够掌握中等手写汉字表中的汉字 250 个。
    □1 完全不符合　　□2 勉强符合　　□3 基本符合　　□4 比较符合
    □5 完全符合

14. 能够使用较为复杂的句式进行语段表达。
    □1 完全不符合　　□2 勉强符合　　□3 基本符合　　□4 比较符合
    □5 完全符合

15. 能够分析常见汉字的结构。
    □1 完全不符合　　□2 勉强符合　　□3 基本符合　　□4 比较符合
    □5 完全符合

16. 在规定时间内，完成一般的叙述性、说明性及简单的议论性等语言材料的写作，字数不低于 450 字。
    □1 完全不符合　　□2 勉强符合　　□3 基本符合　　□4 比较符合
    □5 完全符合

17. 用词较为恰当，句式基本正确，内容比较完整，表达较为通顺。
    □1 完全不符合　　□2 勉强符合　　□3 基本符合　　□4 比较符合
    □5 完全符合

18. 能够完成一般的应用文体写作，格式正确，表达基本规范。
    □1 完全不符合　　□2 勉强符合　　□3 基本符合　　□4 比较符合
    □5 完全符合

▶▶▶ 第二部分：Aligning HSK Level 5 Writing Test with *Chinese Proficiency Grading Standards for International Chinese Language Education*

第 100 题：

请结合这张图片写一篇 80 字左右的短文。

请判断上题，在多大程度上能够考查《国际中文教育中文水平等级标准》5 级所描述的相应写作能力，并点击相应的数字。

19. 能够掌握中等手写汉字表中的汉字 250 个。

　　□1 完全不符合　□2 勉强符合　□3 基本符合　□4 比较符合
　　□5 完全符合

20. 能够使用较为复杂的句式进行语段表达。

　　□1 完全不符合　□2 勉强符合　□3 基本符合　□4 比较符合
　　□5 完全符合

21. 能够分析常见汉字的结构。

　　□1 完全不符合　□2 勉强符合　□3 基本符合　□4 比较符合
　　□5 完全符合

22. 在规定时间内，完成一般的叙述性、说明性及简单的议论性等语言材料的写作，字数不低于 450 字。

　　□1 完全不符合　□2 勉强符合　□3 基本符合　□4 比较符合
　　□5 完全符合

23. 用词较为恰当，句式基本正确，内容比较完整，表达较为通顺。

　　□1 完全不符合　□2 勉强符合　□3 基本符合　□4 比较符合
　　□5 完全符合

24. 能够完成一般的应用文体写作，格式正确，表达基本规范。

　　□1 完全不符合　□2 勉强符合　□3 基本符合　□4 比较符合
　　□5 完全符合

第三套考题
（仅提供第 99 和 100 题）

第 99 题：

请结合下列词语（要全部使用，顺序不分先后），写一篇 80 字左右的短文。

信任　利润　共同　合作　任何

请判断上题，在多大程度上能够考查《国际中文教育中文水平等级标准》5 级所描述的相应写作能力，并点击相应的数字。

25. 能够掌握中等手写汉字表中的汉字 250 个。
    □1 完全不符合　□2 勉强符合　□3 基本符合　□4 比较符合
    □5 完全符合

26. 能够使用较为复杂的句式进行语段表达。
    □1 完全不符合　□2 勉强符合　□3 基本符合　□4 比较符合
    □5 完全符合

27. 能够分析常见汉字的结构。
    □1 完全不符合　□2 勉强符合　□3 基本符合　□4 比较符合
    □5 完全符合

28. 在规定时间内，完成一般的叙述性、说明性及简单的议论性等语言材料的写作，字数不低于 450 字。
    □1 完全不符合　□2 勉强符合　□3 基本符合　□4 比较符合
    □5 完全符合

29. 用词较为恰当，句式基本正确，内容比较完整，表达较为通顺。
    □1 完全不符合　□2 勉强符合　□3 基本符合　□4 比较符合
    □5 完全符合

30. 能够完成一般的应用文体写作，格式正确，表达基本规范。
    □1 完全不符合　□2 勉强符合　□3 基本符合　□4 比较符合
    □5 完全符合

第100题：

请结合这张图片写一篇80字左右的短文。

请判断上题，在多大程度上能够考查《国际中文教育中文水平等级标准》5级所描述的相应写作能力，并点击相应的数字。

31. 能够掌握中等手写汉字表中的汉字250个。
    □1 完全不符合　□2 勉强符合　□3 基本符合　□4 比较符合
    □5 完全符合

32. 能够使用较为复杂的句式进行语段表达。
    □1 完全不符合　□2 勉强符合　□3 基本符合　□4 比较符合
    □5 完全符合

33. 能够分析常见汉字的结构。
    □1 完全不符合　□2 勉强符合　□3 基本符合　□4 比较符合
    □5 完全符合

34. 在规定时间内，完成一般的叙述性、说明性及简单的议论性等语言材料的写作，字数不低于450字。
    □1 完全不符合　□2 勉强符合　□3 基本符合　□4 比较符合
    □5 完全符合

35. 用词较为恰当，句式基本正确，内容比较完整，表达较为通顺。
    □1 完全不符合　□2 勉强符合　□3 基本符合　□4 比较符合
    □5 完全符合

36. 能够完成一般的应用文体写作，格式正确，表达基本规范。
    □1 完全不符合　□2 勉强符合　□3 基本符合　□4 比较符合
    □5 完全符合

Appendix C
问卷1:《国际中文教育中文水平等级标准》与第99题考生文本的关系判断问卷(文本1—6)

尊敬的专家老师:

您好!非常感谢您拨冗参与此次研究!

如您所知,HSK是一项国际化考试,重点考查母语非汉语者运用中文进行交际的能力。于2021年3月正式发布的《国际中文教育中文水平等级标准》是我国首个面向外国汉语学习者,全面描绘评价学习者汉语语言技能和水平的规范标准。

请您运用您的专业知识,认真仔细阅读,完成本问卷中的判断。非常感谢您的合作和帮助。

请您仔细阅读以下内容:

一、数据保密原则:未经本研究负责人同意,不得以泄露、告知、公布、发表、出版、传授、转让或其他任何方式,直接或间接、故意或无意使第三方(非本研究受试)知悉本研究所提供的任何数据及材料;也不得未经本研究负责人同意,随意挪用本研究中所提供的数据和材料。

二、个人信息保护原则:您所填写的相关信息仅用作研究目的,我们不会对外披露任何有关您的个人资料与信息。

我已经阅读了本知情同意书和数据保密协议,理解本研究的数据保密要求,愿意参加此次研究。

受试签名:_____

本问卷列出了:

(1) 6份HSK 5级考题"书写"部分第99题的考生写作文本;

(2)《国际中文教育中文水平等级标准》5级写作描述语(已拆分)。

请您运用自己的专业知识,对这6份考生写作文本在多大程度上能够反映《国际中文教育中文水平等级标准》5级所描述的相应写作能力做出判断,并点击相应的数字。

文本1：

> 99. 现在人们喜欢购物，人们觉得在网上买东西的话一方面可以省时间，别外一方面省麻烦。我觉得他们样式不错的,有人不喜欢购物，这就是舍不得花钱，我感觉这样的习惯不太好我以前好几次购物过了买的东西都正好不大不小。

请判断该考生写作文本，在多大程度上能够反映《国际中文教育中文水平等级标准》5级所描述的相应写作能力，并点击相应的数字。

1. 能够掌握中等手写汉字表中的汉字250个。
   □1 完全不符合　□2 勉强符合　□3 基本符合　□4 比较符合
   □5 完全符合

2. 能够使用较为复杂的句式进行语段表达。
   □1 完全不符合　□2 勉强符合　□3 基本符合　□4 比较符合
   □5 完全符合

3. 能够分析常见汉字的结构。
   □1 完全不符合　□2 勉强符合　□3 基本符合　□4 比较符合
   □5 完全符合

4. 在规定时间内，完成一般的叙述性、说明性及简单的议论性等语言材料的写作，字数不低于450字。
   □1 完全不符合　□2 勉强符合　□3 基本符合　□4 比较符合
   □5 完全符合

5. 用词较为恰当，句式基本正确，内容比较完整，表达较为通顺。
   □1 完全不符合　□2 勉强符合　□3 基本符合　□4 比较符合
   □5 完全符合

6. 能够完成一般的应用文体写作，格式正确，表达基本规范。
   □1 完全不符合　□2 勉强符合　□3 基本符合　□4 比较符合
   □5 完全符合

文本2：

> 99. 一天我和朋友们很多牌去看看这
> 个书他们消说外不想以后我们实际说上
> 我们去吃说饭他级人不很么知以后他
> 去在家知很承人明天他们去去动物回
> 看看动物以后我们回家知吃很多饭

请判断该考生写作文本，在多大程度上能够反映《国际中文教育中文水平等级标准》5级所描述的相应写作能力，并点击相应的数字。

7. 能够掌握中等手写汉字表中的汉字 250 个。
   □1 完全不符合　□2 勉强符合　□3 基本符合　□4 比较符合
   □5 完全符合

8. 能够使用较为复杂的句式进行语段表达。
   □1 完全不符合　□2 勉强符合　□3 基本符合　□4 比较符合
   □5 完全符合

9. 能够分析常见汉字的结构。
   □1 完全不符合　□2 勉强符合　□3 基本符合　□4 比较符合
   □5 完全符合

10. 在规定时间内，完成一般的叙述性、说明性及简单的议论性等语言材料的写作，字数不低于 450 字。
    □1 完全不符合　□2 勉强符合　□3 基本符合　□4 比较符合
    □5 完全符合

11. 用词较为恰当，句式基本正确，内容比较完整，表达较为通顺。
    □1 完全不符合　□2 勉强符合　□3 基本符合　□4 比较符合
    □5 完全符合

12. 能够完成一般的应用文体写作，格式正确，表达基本规范。
    □1 完全不符合　□2 勉强符合　□3 基本符合　□4 比较符合
    □5 完全符合

文本3：

请判断该考生写作文本，在多大程度上能够反映《国际中文教育中文水平等级标准》5级所描述的相应写作能力，并点击相应的数字。

13. 能够掌握中等手写汉字表中的汉字250个。
    □1 完全不符合　□2 勉强符合　□3 基本符合　□4 比较符合
    □5 完全符合

14. 能够使用较为复杂的句式进行语段表达。
    □1 完全不符合　□2 勉强符合　□3 基本符合　□4 比较符合
    □5 完全符合

15. 能够分析常见汉字的结构。
    □1 完全不符合　□2 勉强符合　□3 基本符合　□4 比较符合
    □5 完全符合

16. 在规定时间内，完成一般的叙述性、说明性及简单的议论性等语言材料的写作，字数不低于450字。
    □1 完全不符合　□2 勉强符合　□3 基本符合　□4 比较符合
    □5 完全符合

17. 用词较为恰当，句式基本正确，内容比较完整，表达较为通顺。
    □1 完全不符合　□2 勉强符合　□3 基本符合　□4 比较符合
    □5 完全符合

18. 能够完成一般的应用文体写作，格式正确，表达基本规范。
    □1 完全不符合　□2 勉强符合　□3 基本符合　□4 比较符合
    □5 完全符合

文本4：

> 99. 我的一位好朋友一直很反对健身。因为对锻炼的空闲，我这些朋友就从没有健过身。但是，我天天告诉他健身和锻炼身体是对身体很好的也可以给自己一个更好的身材。我朋友终于克服了不想健身的想法和我一起写出了一个计划。让我太高兴了！

请判断该考生写作文本，在多大程度上能够反映《国际中文教育中文水平等级标准》5级所描述的相应写作能力，并点击相应的数字。

19. 能够掌握中等手写汉字表中的汉字250个。
　　☐1 完全不符合　☐2 勉强符合　☐3 基本符合　☐4 比较符合
　　☐5 完全符合

20. 能够使用较为复杂的句式进行语段表达。
　　☐1 完全不符合　☐2 勉强符合　☐3 基本符合　☐4 比较符合
　　☐5 完全符合

21. 能够分析常见汉字的结构。
　　☐1 完全不符合　☐2 勉强符合　☐3 基本符合　☐4 比较符合
　　☐5 完全符合

22. 在规定时间内，完成一般的叙述性、说明性及简单的议论性等语言材料的写作，字数不低于450字。
　　☐1 完全不符合　☐2 勉强符合　☐3 基本符合　☐4 比较符合
　　☐5 完全符合

23. 用词较为恰当，句式基本正确，内容比较完整，表达较为通顺。
　　☐1 完全不符合　☐2 勉强符合　☐3 基本符合　☐4 比较符合
　　☐5 完全符合

24. 能够完成一般的应用文体写作，格式正确，表达基本规范。
　　☐1 完全不符合　☐2 勉强符合　☐3 基本符合　☐4 比较符合
　　☐5 完全符合

文本5：

> 99. 在生活中，保护环境十分重要。一旦环境受到危险，我们生活也会被伤害。所以我们都要珍惜大自然，它是我们的宝贵。怎么保护它呢？我们要减少使用资源，关灯，电脑之类。我们要把能源其极看重。我们的世界在于大自然。

请判断该考生写作文本，在多大程度上能够反映《国际中文教育中文水平等级标准》5级所描述的相应写作能力，并点击相应的数字。

25. 能够掌握中等手写汉字表中的汉字250个。
    □1 完全不符合　□2 勉强符合　□3 基本符合　□4 比较符合
    □5 完全符合

26. 能够使用较为复杂的句式进行语段表达。
    □1 完全不符合　□2 勉强符合　□3 基本符合　□4 比较符合
    □5 完全符合

27. 能够分析常见汉字的结构。
    □1 完全不符合　□2 勉强符合　□3 基本符合　□4 比较符合
    □5 完全符合

28. 在规定时间内，完成一般的叙述性、说明性及简单的议论性等语言材料的写作，字数不低于450字。
    □1 完全不符合　□2 勉强符合　□3 基本符合　□4 比较符合
    □5 完全符合

29. 用词较为恰当，句式基本正确，内容比较完整，表达较为通顺。
    □1 完全不符合　□2 勉强符合　□3 基本符合　□4 比较符合
    □5 完全符合

30. 能够完成一般的应用文体写作，格式正确，表达基本规范。
    □1 完全不符合　□2 勉强符合　□3 基本符合　□4 比较符合
    □5 完全符合

文本6：

> 99. 今年我终于大学毕业了。我想感谢各位老师。我在母校读书时，就学到了那么多东西，学会思考、分析，提高了我的汉语水平，认识到很多良好的人。总之，很有收获。到现在我们班同学们关系亲切，每次跟他们见面，我的心情就变好一些。

请判断该考生写作文本，在多大程度上能够反映《国际中文教育中文水平等级标准》5级所描述的相应写作能力，并点击相应的数字。

31. 能够掌握中等手写汉字表中的汉字 250 个。
    □1 完全不符合　□2 勉强符合　□3 基本符合　□4 比较符合
    □5 完全符合

32. 能够使用较为复杂的句式进行语段表达。
    □1 完全不符合　□2 勉强符合　□3 基本符合　□4 比较符合
    □5 完全符合

33. 能够分析常见汉字的结构。
    □1 完全不符合　□2 勉强符合　□3 基本符合　□4 比较符合
    □5 完全符合

34. 在规定时间内，完成一般的叙述性、说明性及简单的议论性等语言材料的写作，字数不低于 450 字。
    □1 完全不符合　□2 勉强符合　□3 基本符合　□4 比较符合
    □5 完全符合

35. 用词较为恰当，句式基本正确，内容比较完整，表达较为通顺。
    □1 完全不符合　□2 勉强符合　□3 基本符合　□4 比较符合
    □5 完全符合

36. 能够完成一般的应用文体写作，格式正确，表达基本规范。
    □1 完全不符合　□2 勉强符合　□3 基本符合　□4 比较符合
    □5 完全符合

问卷 2:《国际中文教育中文水平等级标准》与第 100 题考生文本的关系判断问卷(文本 31—36)

尊敬的专家老师:

您好!非常感谢您拨冗参与此次研究!

如您所知,HSK 是一项国际化考试,重点考查母语非汉语者运用中文进行交际的能力。于 2021 年 3 月正式发布的《国际中文教育中文水平等级标准》是我国首个面向外国汉语学习者,全面描绘评价学习者汉语语言技能和水平的规范标准。

请您运用您的专业知识,认真仔细阅读,完成本问卷中的判断。非常感谢您的合作和帮助。

请您仔细阅读以下内容:

一、数据保密原则:未经本研究负责人同意,不得以泄露、告知、公布、发表、出版、传授、转让或其他任何方式,直接或间接、故意或无意使第三方(非本研究受试)知悉本研究所提供的任何数据及材料;也不得未经本研究负责人同意,随意挪用本研究中所提供的数据和材料。

二、个人信息保护原则:您所填写的相关信息仅用作研究目的,我们不会对外披露任何有关您的个人资料与信息。

我已经阅读了本知情同意书和数据保密协议,理解本研究的数据保密要求,愿意参加此次研究。

受试签名:＿＿＿＿＿＿＿＿＿＿

本问卷列出了:

(1) 6 份 HSK 5 级考题"书写"部分第 100 题的考生写作文本;
(2)《国际中文教育中文水平等级标准》5 级写作描述语(已拆分)。

请您运用自己的专业知识,对这 6 份考生写作文本在多大程度上能够反映《国际中文教育中文水平等级标准》5 级所描述的相应写作能力做出判断,并点击相应的数字。

文本 31：

> 他们今天做了非多的菜，这个菜真想阿！四个人做了四个，正在大家都怕照片。他们要很快吃，肚子也很饿了。每个人有自己的拿手菜，这样在家里能做的可以道时吃也不有每天出门。准备在家里想吃什么就吃什么。

请判断该考生写作文本，在多大程度上能够反映《国际中文教育中文水平等级标准》5 级所描述的相应写作能力，并点击相应的数字。

1. 能够掌握中等手写汉字表中的汉字 250 个。
   □1 完全不符合　□2 勉强符合　□3 基本符合　□4 比较符合
   □5 完全符合

2. 能够使用较为复杂的句式进行语段表达。
   □1 完全不符合　□2 勉强符合　□3 基本符合　□4 比较符合
   □5 完全符合

3. 能够分析常见汉字的结构。
   □1 完全不符合　□2 勉强符合　□3 基本符合　□4 比较符合
   □5 完全符合

4. 在规定时间内，完成一般的叙述性、说明性及简单的议论性等语言材料的写作，字数不低于 450 字。
   □1 完全不符合　□2 勉强符合　□3 基本符合　□4 比较符合
   □5 完全符合

5. 用词较为恰当，句式基本正确，内容比较完整，表达较为通顺。
   □1 完全不符合　□2 勉强符合　□3 基本符合　□4 比较符合
   □5 完全符合

6. 能够完成一般的应用文体写作，格式正确，表达基本规范。
   □1 完全不符合　□2 勉强符合　□3 基本符合　□4 比较符合
   □5 完全符合

文本32：

请判断该考生写作文本，在多大程度上能够反映《国际中文教育中文水平等级标准》5级所描述的相应写作能力，并点击相应的数字。

7. 能够掌握中等手写汉字表中的汉字250个。
   □1 完全不符合　□2 勉强符合　□3 基本符合　□4 比较符合
   □5 完全符合

8. 能够使用较为复杂的句式进行语段表达。
   □1 完全不符合　□2 勉强符合　□3 基本符合　□4 比较符合
   □5 完全符合

9. 能够分析常见汉字的结构。
   □1 完全不符合　□2 勉强符合　□3 基本符合　□4 比较符合
   □5 完全符合

10. 在规定时间内，完成一般的叙述性、说明性及简单的议论性等语言材料的写作，字数不低于450字。
    □1 完全不符合　□2 勉强符合　□3 基本符合　□4 比较符合
    □5 完全符合

11. 用词较为恰当，句式基本正确，内容比较完整，表达较为通顺。
    □1 完全不符合　□2 勉强符合　□3 基本符合　□4 比较符合
    □5 完全符合

12. 能够完成一般的应用文体写作，格式正确，表达基本规范。
    □1 完全不符合　□2 勉强符合　□3 基本符合　□4 比较符合
    □5 完全符合

文本 33：

> 我一八岁时决定去中国当留学生。在中国，我住了在一个商学校附近的房间。但是，因为当时是我第一次自己一个人住，我遇到问题时常常要跟爸爸打电话找决郎。我很感谢爸爸那时候的帮助，一直让我慢慢得变能干。

请判断该考生写作文本，在多大程度上能够反映《国际中文教育中文水平等级标准》5 级所描述的相应写作能力，并点击相应的数字。

13. 能够掌握中等手写汉字表中的汉字 250 个。
    □1 完全不符合　□2 勉强符合　□3 基本符合　□4 比较符合
    □5 完全符合

14. 能够使用较为复杂的句式进行语段表达。
    □1 完全不符合　□2 勉强符合　□3 基本符合　□4 比较符合
    □5 完全符合

15. 能够分析常见汉字的结构。
    □1 完全不符合　□2 勉强符合　□3 基本符合　□4 比较符合
    □5 完全符合

16. 在规定时间内，完成一般的叙述性、说明性及简单的议论性等语言材料的写作，字数不低于 450 字。
    □1 完全不符合　□2 勉强符合　□3 基本符合　□4 比较符合
    □5 完全符合

17. 用词较为恰当，句式基本正确，内容比较完整，表达较为通顺。
    □1 完全不符合　□2 勉强符合　□3 基本符合　□4 比较符合
    □5 完全符合

18. 能够完成一般的应用文体写作，格式正确，表达基本规范。
    □1 完全不符合　□2 勉强符合　□3 基本符合　□4 比较符合
    □5 完全符合

文本34：

> 100. 明天是我妈妈的生日，要四十五岁了。可是因为我姐姐出国学习她就不能跟我们一家过我妈的生日所以我妈不高兴。她很想我姐。但是我们一家刚要唱生日歌时，我姐姐就突然走到屋子里面告诉我们她刚下飞机坐车过来的。我妈妈非常的高兴！

请判断该考生写作文本，在多大程度上能够反映《国际中文教育中文水平等级标准》5级所描述的相应写作能力，并点击相应的数字。

19. 能够掌握中等手写汉字表中的汉字250个。
    □1 完全不符合　□2 勉强符合　□3 基本符合　□4 比较符合
    □5 完全符合

20. 能够使用较为复杂的句式进行语段表达。
    □1 完全不符合　□2 勉强符合　□3 基本符合　□4 比较符合
    □5 完全符合

21. 能够分析常见汉字的结构。
    □1 完全不符合　□2 勉强符合　□3 基本符合　□4 比较符合
    □5 完全符合

22. 在规定时间内，完成一般的叙述性、说明性及简单的议论性等语言材料的写作，字数不低于450字。
    □1 完全不符合　□2 勉强符合　□3 基本符合　□4 比较符合
    □5 完全符合

23. 用词较为恰当，句式基本正确，内容比较完整，表达较为通顺。
    □1 完全不符合　□2 勉强符合　□3 基本符合　□4 比较符合
    □5 完全符合

24. 能够完成一般的应用文体写作，格式正确，表达基本规范。
    □1 完全不符合　□2 勉强符合　□3 基本符合　□4 比较符合
    □5 完全符合

文本 35：

> 100. 在这张图片上有一个小女孩子。她正在弹钢琴。很可能她有钢琴辅导班。她的父母说不定觉得她有能力，要培养孩子的特长。弹钢琴对她来说很有趣，因为小女孩子的表情十分专心。在她的旁边现在没有老师，所以女孩儿的能力一定很高。

请判断该考生写作文本，在多大程度上能够反映《国际中文教育中文水平等级标准》5级所描述的相应写作能力，并点击相应的数字。

25. 能够掌握中等手写汉字表中的汉字 250 个。
    □1 完全不符合　□2 勉强符合　□3 基本符合　□4 比较符合
    □5 完全符合

26. 能够使用较为复杂的句式进行语段表达。
    □1 完全不符合　□2 勉强符合　□3 基本符合　□4 比较符合
    □5 完全符合

27. 能够分析常见汉字的结构。
    □1 完全不符合　□2 勉强符合　□3 基本符合　□4 比较符合
    □5 完全符合

28. 在规定时间内，完成一般的叙述性、说明性及简单的议论性等语言材料的写作，字数不低于 450 字。
    □1 完全不符合　□2 勉强符合　□3 基本符合　□4 比较符合
    □5 完全符合

29. 用词较为恰当，句式基本正确，内容比较完整，表达较为通顺。
    □1 完全不符合　□2 勉强符合　□3 基本符合　□4 比较符合
    □5 完全符合

30. 能够完成一般的应用文体写作，格式正确，表达基本规范。
    □1 完全不符合　□2 勉强符合　□3 基本符合　□4 比较符合
    □5 完全符合

文本36：

> 100. 这张照片上我们可以看到个年轻女性。她的卫生间里的水龙头出了问题，她就无法洗手。她看上去比较辛苦。她自己不知道该怎办，觉得很无奈。她立刻给父亲打电话，询问他一下。我希望她会解决这个问题克服困难。

请判断该考生写作文本，在多大程度上能够反映《国际中文教育中文水平等级标准》5级所描述的相应写作能力，并点击相应的数字。

31. 能够掌握中等手写汉字表中的汉字250个。
    □1 完全不符合　□2 勉强符合　□3 基本符合　□4 比较符合
    □5 完全符合

32. 能够使用较为复杂的句式进行语段表达。
    □1 完全不符合　□2 勉强符合　□3 基本符合　□4 比较符合
    □5 完全符合

33. 能够分析常见汉字的结构。
    □1 完全不符合　□2 勉强符合　□3 基本符合　□4 比较符合
    □5 完全符合

34. 在规定时间内，完成一般的叙述性、说明性及简单的议论性等语言材料的写作，字数不低于450字。
    □1 完全不符合　□2 勉强符合　□3 基本符合　□4 比较符合
    □5 完全符合

35. 用词较为恰当，句式基本正确，内容比较完整，表达较为通顺。
    □1 完全不符合　□2 勉强符合　□3 基本符合　□4 比较符合
    □5 完全符合

36. 能够完成一般的应用文体写作，格式正确，表达基本规范。
    □1 完全不符合　□2 勉强符合　□3 基本符合　□4 比较符合
    □5 完全符合

Appendix D
访谈提纲

第一部分：《国际中文教育中文水平等级标准》与 HSK 考题的关系

1. 总体而言，您觉得第 99 题（第 100）考题能和《国际中文教育中文水平等级标准》相匹配吗？
2. 您觉得描述语 1 和第 99 题（第 100 题）考题间的匹配程度如何？为什么？
3. 您觉得描述语 2 和第 99 题（第 100 题）考题间的匹配程度如何？为什么？
4. 您觉得描述语 3 和第 99 题（第 100 题）考题间的匹配程度如何？为什么？
5. 您觉得描述语 4 和第 99 题（第 100 题）考题间的匹配程度如何？为什么？
6. 您觉得描述语 5 和第 99 题（第 100 题）考题间的匹配程度如何？为什么？
7. 您觉得描述语 6 和第 99 题（第 100 题）考题间的匹配程度如何？为什么？

第二部分：《国际中文教育中文水平等级标准》与 HSK 考生文本的关系

1. 总体而言，您觉得第 99 题（第 100 题）的考生文本和《国际中文教育中文水平等级标准》相匹配吗？
2. 您觉得描述语 1 和第 99 题（第 100 题）的考生文本间的匹配程度如何？为什么？
3. 您觉得描述语 2 和第 99 题（第 100 题）的考生文本间的匹配程度如何？为什么？
4. 您觉得描述语 3 和第 99 题（第 100 题）的考生文本间的匹配程度如何？为什么？
5. 您觉得描述语 4 和第 99 题（第 100 题）的考生文本间的匹配程度如何？为什么？
6. 您觉得描述语 5 和第 99 题（第 100 题）的考生文本间的匹配程度如何？为什么？
7. 您觉得描述语 6 和第 99 题（第 100 题）的考生文本间的匹配程度如何？为什么？